The Plant

MW01289349

Missionary Churches

John L. Nevius

BY

REV. JOHN L. NEVIUS, D.D.

LATE MISSIONARY TO CHINA

FOREIGN MISSION LIBRARY

156 FIFTH AVENUE

NEW YORK

NOTE PREFATORY TO THIRD EDITION

This little book first appeared as a series of articles which were published in the "Chinese Recorder" in 1885. They immediately aroused great interest in a missionary scheme about which little was generally known, except that it was very successful. So great was the demand for these letters by the late Dr. Nevius, that they were reprinted in book form by the Presbyterian Press, Shanghai, in 1886. The interest in the discussion having spread to this country, a second edition was prepared by Mr. W. H. Grant and published in the "Foreign Mission Library" of the Presbyterian Board, New York.

During the years that have intervened since their first appearance, Dr. Nevius's methods have been successfully tested in other fields—notably and most fruitfully in Korea—and have been very highly endorsed by many board secretaries. While it is but fair to other theories of missionary work to say, that even in Dr. Nevius's own field his plans were not wholly satisfactory, and that from 1885 to the present year some Chinese missionaries have strongly argued against them, it is also true that no single scheme hitherto published promises so well to meet the pressing emergencies of the present time.

When every dollar must do its utmost good with the least harm, and when candidates for the foreign field are studying as never before the varied aspects of missions, it was deemed best to bring out a new edition for the special use of mission study classes of the Student Volunteer Movement for Foreign Missions. The present book differs from the preceding edition in its title, in the omission of a few lines having local and temporary interest only, and in the chapter and paragraph divisions, which have been made to correspond to other books of the Movement. It may be said with reference to these latter changes, the bold-faced **Clarendon type** indicates main divisions, the paragraphs headed by Arabic numerals constitute subordinate divisions, and other paragraphs subdivisions. Numerals have been employed for the convenience of students and leaders of classes who use an analytical outline—published elsewhere—in preparing for the class.

NEW YORK, March 1, 1899.

CONTENTS

PAGE

I. THE OLD SYSTEM CRITICISED 8
Introductory. 8
Old System vs. the New. 8
Spirit and Attitude in this Discussion. 10
Old Method a Natural One. 11
Objections to the Old Method. 13
II. HOW TO DEAL WITH NEW CONVERTS? 19
Abiding in the Old Calling. 19
Importance of Precedents. 22
Nature of the Church and Its Development. 25
Test Necessary before Advancement. 25
Necessity of Training. 27
Commit Converts to the Lord. 28
III. ORIGIN AND GROWTH OF STATIONS IN CENTRAL
SHAN-TUNG 29
General View of the Shan-tung Work. 29
Relations of the Missionary Helpers and Leaders. 31
Principle Underlying Station Organization. 31
Instruction of Inquirers and Church Members. 34
Bible or Training Classes. 38
Results to Station Members. 40
Manner in which Stations are Propagated. 41
Classes to which Our Church Members Belong. 42
Persecution. 43
Sabbath Observance. 44
Discipline. 46
Contributions. 49
Schools. 49
Men Employed and Incidental Expenses. 50
Summary and Forecast. 51
IV. ORGANIZATION OF STATIONS, PRESENT AND
PROSPECTIVE 53

Varying Views Concerning Church Organization. 53
Scripture Teachings as to the Best System for China. 56
Experience Proves the Wisdom of Scripture Teachings. 65
V. BEGINNING WORK 68
The Study of the Language. 68
Beginning Direct Missionary Work. 71
Independent Individual Work. 73
Itinerating. 74
Assistants or Helpers. 75
How Shall We Reach the People? 77
How Best To Expend One's Time? 79
Missionaries but Instruments in Spiritual Work.......................81
Personal Experience in Beginning Work in Shan-Tung............82
How May We Best Get Out of "Old Ruts"? 84

I. THE OLD SYSTEM CRITICISED

Introductory.

A request from the Editor of the "Chinese Recorder" to prepare for publication some account of the character and results of our country work in Shan-tung, and private letters from various sources asking for information on the same general subject, have furnished evidence that such information may be of service, more especially to young missionaries.

The interest which has been taken in our work in central Shan-tung by missionaries in other provinces is due no doubt to the fact that we have to some extent adopted new principles and methods. It is too early to determine what the final issue of this new departure will be, but perhaps not too soon to deprive some important lessons from present facts and experiences and results so far as developed.

Old System vs. the New.

1. The adoption of the new plan having been the result in many cases of difficulties and discouragements in connection with the previous one, our present position will be best understood by considering the two systems, which may for the sake of convenience be called the Old and the New, in their relation to each other. In the following pages we will present the reasons which have led to the disuse of the former, the adoption of the latter, and the manner in which the transition has been made.

2. I think it may be stated that forty years ago, missionaries in China, with few if any exceptions, followed the Old Method. The change of view has not been sudden but gradual and always in the

same direction, producing a continually widening and more irreconcilable breach between the two systems. There is now a prevailing disposition in our part of the field, at least among the missionaries of the American Presbyterian, the English Baptist, and the American Baptist Missions, to follow the New Plan, which may still, however, be regarded as in a formative and tentative stage of development.

3. These two systems may be distinguished in general by the former depending largely on paid native agency, while the latter deprecates and seeks to minimize such agency. Perhaps an equally correct and more generally acceptable statement of the difference would be, that, while both alike seek ultimately the establishment of independent, self-reliant, and aggressive native churches, the Old System strives by the use of foreign funds to foster and stimulate the growth of the native churches in the first stage of their development, and then gradually to discontinue the use of such funds; while those who adopt the New System think that the desired object may be best attained by applying principles of independence and self-reliance from the beginning. The difference between these two theories may be more clearly seen in their outward practical working. The Old uses freely, and as far as practicable, the more advanced and intelligent of the native church members in the capacity of paid *colporteurs*, Bible agents, evangelists, or heads of stations; while the New proceeds on the assumption that the persons employed in these various capacities would be more useful in the end by being left in their original homes and employments.

4. The relative advantages of these systems may be determined by two tests—adaptability to the end in view, and Scripture authority. Some missionaries regard the principles and practices adopted by the Apostles in early times and recorded in the Scriptures as inapplicable to our changed circumstances in China in this nineteenth century. Leaving the consideration of this question for the present, it will no doubt be acknowledged by all, that any plan which will bear the application of the two tests of adaptability and Scripture authority, has a much stronger claim upon our regard and acceptance than a plan which can only claim the sanction of one test.

As a matter of fact the change of views of not a few of the older missionaries in China is due, not to theoretical, but practical considerations. The Old System has been gradually discarded because it did not work, or because it worked evil. In my own case I can say that every change in opinion was brought about by a long and painful experience; and conclusions arrived at have been only a confirmation of what I regard as the teachings of the Bible. The same conclusions might have been reached with an immense economy of time and labor by simply following the authoritative guide which God has given us. If the New System be indeed sanctioned by Scripture authority as well as by the tests of practical adaptability and use, an exchange or reversal in the application of the names New and Old would be more in accordance with fact.

Spirit and Attitude in this Discussion.

1. In stating what I regard as serious objections to previous methods, I may come in conflict with the opinions of my brethren. I desire, however, to write, not in the spirit of a critic, much less of a censor, but as one earnestly desirous of knowing the truth. I have in former years to a considerable extent believed in and worked upon the Old System, and what I have to say by way of strictures on it may be considered as a confession of personal error, rather than of fault-finding with others. Foreigners who have come to China to devote themselves to business or diplomacy have made their mistakes; it is not strange, but rather to be expected, that we should make ours. Let us acknowledge them and profit by them.

2. I am aware that it is possible to state facts in such a way that the impression given will be a false one, and conclusions arrived at misleading. It will be my earnest endeavor in the ensuring papers, not only to give facts and honest conclusions therefrom, but to present them in such a way that the impression given will be, if not always an agreeable one, yet strictly true and just.

3. I wish further to disclaim all assumption of ability to speak authoritatively on this subject, as though I had myself reached its final solution. The effect of a long experience in mission work has been in my case to deepen a sense of incompetency, and to excite wonder in remembering the inconsiderate realness and self-dependence of a quarter of a century ago. Still, though we may not

feel competent to give advice, we may at least give a word of warning. Though we may not have learned what to do in certain cases and under certain circumstances, it is not much to have learned what not to do, and to tread cautiously where we do not know the way, and to regard with hesitation and suspicion any preconceived opinion which we know to be of doubtful expediency, especially if it is authorized by Scripture teaching and example?

4. I gladly recognize the fact that the use of other methods, depending to a greater or less extent on paid agents, has in many cases been followed with most happy results; and that to a certain extent tried and proved native agents must be employed. I do not wish to make invidious comparisons, much less to decide where the happy mean in using a paid agency lies.

5. Let us bear in mind that the best methods cannot do away with the difficulties in our work which come from the world, the flesh, and the devil, but bad methods may multiply and intensify them. For unavoidable difficulties we are not responsible; for those which arise from disregard of the teachings of Scripture and experience we are.

6. Let us also remember that while in undertaking the momentous task committed to us, we should by the study of the Scriptures, prayer for divine guidance, and comparison of our varied views and experiences, seek to know what is the best method of work; still, the best method without the presence of our Master and the Spirit of all Truth will be unavailing. A bad method may be so bad as to make it unreasonable to expect God's blessing in connection with it; a right and Scriptural method, if we trust in it, as our principal ground of hope, might be followed for a lifetime without any good results.

With this much by way of introduction, I now propose to consider more objections to the Old Method.

Old Method a Natural One.

1. It is only natural that missionaries should at first seek and employ many native agents. They are anxious for immediate results, and home societies and the home churches are as impatient to hear of results as missionaries are to report them. No communications from

the field seem so indicative of progress, and are so calculated to call forth commendation and generous contributions as the announcement that native laborers have been obtained, and are preaching the gospel. While the missionary himself is for months or years debarred from evangelistic work by his ignorance of the language, a native agency stands waiting his employ. His circumstances and his wishes add strong emphasis to the oft-repeated truism, "China must be evangelized by the Chinese." So urgent seems the necessity to obtain native assistants, that if such as he would like are not forthcoming, he is glad to avail himself of such as he can get. How many of us have thought in connection with some specially interesting inquirer, even before he is baptized, "What a capital assistant that man may make."

2. While the circumstances of the missionary furnish the strongest motives to induce him to multiply native agents as fast as possible, the circumstances of the natives naturally and very strongly lead to the same result. The dense population of this country, and the sharp struggle for existence which it necessitates, have developed in the Chinaman a singular aptitude for finding and using ways and means for making a living. The comparatively expensive mode of life, as a rule absolutely necessary for foreigners, in order to live in China with any reasonable hope of health and usefulness, naturally suggests the idea to the native that so intimate a relation as that which subsists between a teacher and his disciples will in this case undoubtedly prove a profitable one. The Famine Relief work in the northern provinces left the impression that foreigners have money in abundance, and are very ready to give it to those in need; and there are many about us now as much in need as some who received aid during the famine. It is not strange, but only human, that natives under these circumstances should see their opportunity and make the most of it.

3. With these strong motives in the minds of the missionaries and natives conspiring to the same result, it is not without excuse that we should have fallen into what I now believe is a serious mistake, utterly unaware of the danger and injury to the mission cause which ten, twenty or thirty years of experience have disclosed. In this opinion I am not alone; and it is a significant fact that those who hold it, are for the most part persons who have had a long experience on

mission ground. To some, these lessons have come too late to be of much service to them individually, but they will be none the less useful to those who are willing to profit by the experiences of others.

4. I fully recognize the fact that the employment and pay of native laborers is, under suitable circumstances, legitimate and desirable, as much so as the employment and pay of foreigners. Here, however, the important questions arise, who shall be employed, and when and how they shall be employed? These questions will come up for consideration in the course of this series of articles.

Objections to the Old Method.

The following are some of the objections to what we have agreed to call the "Old System":

1. Making paid agents of new converts affects injuriously the stations with which they are connected.

A well-informed and influential man, perhaps the leading spirit in a new station, is one who can be ill-spared. His removal may be most disastrous to the station, and he himself may never find elsewhere such an opportunity for doing good. I have in mind four persons who about twenty-eight years ago gave great promise of usefulness in their homes in connection with our out-stations in Ning-po. While working with their hands in their several callings they bore testimony to the truth wherever they went, and were exciting great interest in their own neighborhoods. It was not long, however, before these men were employed, one by one mission, another by another, and the interest in Christianity in and about their homes ceased. It is to be hoped that they did some good in the positions which they afterward occupied, but I have not been able to learn of any one of them, that his after career was a specially useful one. I refer to these cases not as unusual and exceptional. I could add many others from Chê-chiang and Shan-tung, and I doubt not that similar instances will occur to the minds of most missionaries who read this paper.

The injury to a station in these cases does not consist simply in the loss of the man's influence for good; positive evil is introduced. Envy, jealousy and dissatisfaction with their lot are very apt to be excited in the minds of those who are left. Others think that they also should be employed, if not as preachers, as servants, or in some other capacity. It would be a less serious matter if this feeling could be confined to the station where it originates, but unfortunately it extends to other places and there produces the same injurious effects. The religious interest which passed like a wave over the neighborhood, gives place to another wave of excitement, and the topics of conversation are now place and pay. The man employed has lost very much the character he bore as a disinterested worker for the spiritual good of others, and is now likely to be regarded by many as a kind of employ-agent who ought to use his influence to get them places.

2. Making a paid agent of a new convert often proves an injury to him personally.

He is placed in a position unfavorable to the development of a strong, healthy, Christian character. Some of these men, originally farmers, shopkeepers, peddlers or laborers in the fields, find themselves advanced to a position for which they are by previous habits and training unsuited. The long gown and the affected scholarly air are not becoming to them, and they naturally lose the respect of their neighbors and their influence over them. Men who were self-reliant and aggressive in their original positions, now perform their routine labors in a formal and perfunctory manner. Some, on the other hand, are puffed up with pride and self-conceit, and become arrogant and offensive. Here again I am not theorizing, but speaking from experience, and could multiply cases—as I presume most missionaries could—of deterioration of character in both directions above indicated.

No doubt the employment of some of these men has been followed by good results, but it is still a question whether they might not have accomplished more had they been left where they were found. Some of them have proved most unsatisfactory to their employers, but are retained in their places from year to year, because it seems an injustice to send them back to a mode of life for which they have become unfitted. Others have been dismissed from service, and returned to their homes disappointed and aggrieved; while not a few when they have been dropped as employees have dropped their Christianity, brought reproach upon the cause of Christ, become the enemies of the Church, and given evidence that they were only hirelings—never fit to be enrolled either as preachers or as church members.

3. The Old System makes it difficult to judge between the true and false, whether as preachers or as church members.

That the Chinese are adepts in dissembling, no one who has been long in China will deny. The fact that not a few who were earnest preachers have fallen away when they have ceased to be employed has already been referred to. How many others there are now in employ whose professions are suspended on their pay no one can tell. The Chinese are close analysts of character, and know how to adapt themselves to circumstances and individuals. They are less apt to deceive their own people than foreigners, and less apt to deceive others than those by whom they are employed. The desire that the native preacher may prove a true man biases the judgment. Doubtless the man employed is often self-deceived.

I have had a considerable number of intelligent, and to all appearances sincere Christians, connected with my stations, who fell back and left the Church when they found they were not to be employed. These and a still larger number of inquirers, who learned during the time of their probation that there was very little hope of getting place and pay and fell back before they were baptized, would in all probability, if their desire for employment had been gratified, be found to-day in the Church, sustaining perhaps a fair reputation as preachers or evangelists.

What lesson are we to learn from these facts and experiences? Is it not this, that so long as a free use is made of new converts as paid preachers, we deprive ourselves of one of the most effective means of separating the chaff from the wheat, and of assuring ourselves that the men we are employing are what we hope they are, and that we are not building, or vainly-attempting to build, on a bad foundation.

4. The Employment System tends to excite a mercenary spirit, and to increase the number of mercenary Christians.

Of course we fully admit that many paid agents are sincere, earnest men and that they bring into the Church sincere and earnest believers, some perhaps who would not otherwise be reached. We are here simply pointing out an evil influence and tendency which are connected with one system and avoided by the other. A man will sometimes be found who will listen to a native preacher, apparently much interested, but knowing and caring very little about what is said. When he finds an opportunity, he obtains from the preacher, directly or indirectly, a knowledge of what pay he gets and how he obtained his position. This man perhaps becomes a diligent student of the Scriptures and passes an excellent examination as a candidate for baptism; but he is interested in Christianity only as a means to an end. When this mercenary spirit enters a church, it has a wonderful self-propagating power and follows the universal law of propagating after its kind. The mercenary preacher, whether paid or hoping to be paid, as naturally draws to himself others of like affinities as a magnet attracts iron filings.

In one of the districts of this province there seemed a few years since to be an unusual religious awakening. The interest spread from town to town, the number of inquirers was large, and hundreds of apparently sincere believers were gathered into the Church. It was afterward found that the movement was due largely to mercenary motives of different kinds, both in the propagating agents, and in those who were influenced by them. That district now seems to be struck with a blight. The larger part of those who were received are now excommunicated or under discipline; a very unfavorable impression has been made upon the people generally, and persons sincerely interested in the truth are kept back from seeking a connection with the Church by the unworthy examples of its members. In this district, Shin-kuang, there is little hope of anything being accomplished until after the pruning process has been carried still farther, and we can make a new and better beginning. It is much easier to get unworthy members into the Church than it is to get them out of it, and very little good can be accomplished while they hang upon it as an incubus.

5. The Employment System tends to stop the voluntary work of unpaid agents.

The question naturally arises in the mind of the new convert. "If other persons are paid for preaching why should not I be?" Under the influence of jealousy and discontent it is easy to go a step farther and say, "If the missionary is so blind or so unjust as not to see or acknowledge my claims to be employed as others are, I will leave the work of spreading Christianity to those who are paid for it." This again is not an imaginary case but a common experience. It is evident that the two systems are mutually antagonistic, and whenever an attempt is made to carry them on together, the voluntary system labors under almost insurmountable difficulties. This is a serious objection to the Old System, that it stands in the way of the other, and makes the success of it well-nigh impossible.

6. The Old System tends to lower the character and lessen the influence of the missionary enterprise, both in the eyes of foreigners and natives.

The opprobrious epithet, "Rice Christians," has gained almost universal currency in the East, as expressive of the foreigners' estimate of the actual results of missionary work. This unfavorable judgment, formed by those who are supposed, as eye-witnesses, to have good grounds for it, finds its way to Christian nations in the West, who support missions, and prejudices the missionary cause in the opinion of those who would otherwise be its sympathetic supporters. It is a serious question how far missionaries are to blame for this. While we resent as false the sweeping generalization which would include all Christians in China, or the larger part of them, in this category, it is worse than useless to ignore the readiness of large classes of Chinamen to become "Rice Christians," and the difficulty of determining who do, and who do not, belong to this class. We must also admit the fact, that not a few of those who have found their way into the Church have proved, after years of trial, to be only "Rice Christians." The idea of getting rid of such altogether is undoubtedly a fallacious one. They have been connected with the Church, and probably will be, in all lands and in every age. Still, as this reproach has resulted largely from the fact that hitherto a considerable proportion of native Christians have "eaten the missionary's rice," one effective way for removing the reproach is obvious.

The injurious effects of the paid-agent system on the mass of the Chinese population outside of the Church, are perhaps still greater. The general opinion of the Chinaman as to the motive of one of his countrymen in propagating a foreign religion, is that it is a mercenary one. When he learns that the native preacher is in fact paid by foreigners, he is confirmed in his judgment. What the motive is which actuates the foreign missionary, a motive so strong that he is willing to waste life and money in what seems a fruitless enterprise, he is left to imagine. The most common explanation is that it is a covert scheme for buying adherents with a view to political movements inimical to the state. Of course it is supposed that no loyal native will have anything to do with such a movement. If the Chinaman is told that this enterprise is prompted by disinterested motives, and intended for the good of his people, he is incredulous. Simple professions and protestations have little weight with him, in comparison with his own interpretation of facts. Observing that in some of our stations only those who are employed and paid remain firm in their adherence to the foreigner, while not a few of the others fall back, his opinion is still further confirmed; and he looks on with quiet complacency and rallies his unsuccessful neighbors on their having fallen behind their competitors in their scramble for money. Here again I am not imagining what may happen in the future, but am stating what has actually occurred. The result is that many well-disposed Chinamen of the better classes, who might be brought under Christian influences, are repelled, and those who actually find their way into the Church are composed largely of two opposite classes—those whose honest convictions are so strong that they outweigh and overcome all obstacles, and unworthy persons to whom that feature in mission work which we are controverting is its chief attraction.

Now we readily admit that whatever course we may take, the Chinese in general will still regard us as foreign emissaries, our religion as a feint and our converts as mercenaries. What we deprecate is gratuitously furnishing what will be regarded as conclusive evidence that these unfavorable opinions are well founded. Our enemies are sufficiently formidable without our giving them an unnecessary advantage. The obstacles which oppose us are sufficiently appalling without our adding to them and in this way postponing the time of final success.

The above are some of the principal objections which may be urged against the paid-agent scheme. We will next consider what we regard as a better and more Scriptural way.

II. HOW TO DEAL WITH NEW CONVERTS?

The reception of first converts in any mission is an epoch fruitful of consequences for good and evil. The course pursued at this time will establish precedents, and in a great measure fix the policy and determine the character of the Church of the future. How then shall these first converts be dealt with? To this weighty question the Scriptures furnish us some ready answers.

Abiding in the Old Calling.

1. The command of 1 Cor. vii. 20, "Let each man abide in that calling wherein he was called," is repeated in a different form in the twenty-fourth verse of the same chapter, "Brethren, let each man, wherein he was called, therein abide with God." This Apostolic injunction we are further told was ordained "for all the Churches." It teaches most emphatically that Christianity should not disturb the social relations of its adherents, but requires them to be content with their lot, and to illustrate the Gospel in the spheres of life in which they are called. How many of us have given these passages of Scripture that weight of authority which they deserve? How many of us have realized that in taking untried Christians out of the positions in which God has called them and making evangelists of them, we may be literally, though unconsciously, opposing a divine purpose. Such a course directly tends to unsettle the minds of new converts and excites the very feelings of restlessness and discontent which this command seems specially designed to prevent.

2. It may be objected that the literal carrying out of this injunction would prevent missionaries ever employing any native assistants, and would in fact have prevented our coming to China or

entering the ministry. This objection, so far as it has any weight, lies against the Scripture itself. It may be remarked, however, that all Scripture commands are limited and conditioned by other Scripture teachings and are to be interpreted by them. This passage does not determine whether a man is to abide where he is called permanently or only temporarily. This is a question to be left to the future. Special providences afterward may indicate a further and different divine purpose no less clearly. So Paul did not hesitate, when the proper time had come, to remove Timothy from Lystra, and there was no inconsistency in his doing so.

As for ourselves, we entered the ministry because we believed we had a divine call to it; and the Church has sent us to China because it concurred in this opinion, and considered our characters sufficiently tested and proved to warrant our being sent forth to preach the Gospel, with a reasonable assurance that we had renounced worldly aims and worldly advantages to give our lives to the service of Christ. All we insist on is that the same principles and the same prudence should be used in dealing with the Chinese.

3. In determining whether this command to let every man abide in his calling is applicable and binding at present, it is undoubtedly legitimate to inquire whether there may not be special reasons in this present time which overrule and annul it. I can think of none except such as we may regard as growing out of our special circumstances. For instance, we may have been praying for laborers for the "great harvest," or more specifically that God would give us a native agent to occupy an important station at _____, and we say: "Is not this the man God has sent for this very object?" We should not forget, however, that when this injunction was given there was a great need of workers and as many important places were waiting to be occupied as now.

The object we all have in view is of course to secure the greatest usefulness of the convert, and the greatest good to the common cause. Now if the young Christian seems to have qualifications for making a good evangelist, is he not just the man wanted to develop the work where he is? And will not further experience at home fit him all the better for doing other work to which he may be called in the future, when perhaps he may be spared from his station without its suffering in consequence? God's designs with reference to this man are wiser than ours. Let us wait for those designs to develop, as they surely will, and follow carefully as we are led.

4. Other passages of Scripture place our duty in this matter in a still clearer light. "Not a novice, lest being puffed he fall into the condemnation of the devil." By one rash and unauthorized step we may inflict an irreparable injury on the person in whom we are so much interested, and destroy all hopes of his future usefulness. Again, "Be not many teachers, my brethren, knowing that we shall receive heavier judgment." This is a warning to those would-be teachers, and may be applied with equal force to those who would gratuitously assume the responsibility of recommending and employing teachers, without sufficient Scriptural grounds for doing so. Again we are taught: "Lay hands hastily on no man, neither be partaker of other men's sins; keep thyself pure." The pertinency of these passages is too obvious to require lengthened remarks.

Importance of Precedents.

1. The Chinese are remarkable for their tendency to follow a fixed routine, and to be governed by precedents. If the first convert is soon employed, those who follow will expect to be also. If the first station is supplied with a chapel, succeeding ones will require the same, and so on indefinitely. As a matter of precedent, the question as to whether the Gospel shall be first introduced by the instrumentality of paid or unpaid agents is of such importance as to deserve very careful attention. Here again we get light from Scripture. Nothing is more strikingly characteristic of the missionary methods of the Apostle Paul than his purpose to preach the Gospel freely or "without charge." He gives us very clearly his reason for doing this. "For yourselves know how ye ought to imitate us: for we behaved not ourselves disorderly among you; neither did we eat bread for nought at any man's hand, but in labor and travail, working night and day, that we might not burden any of you: not because we have not the right, but to make ourselves an example unto you, that ye should imitate us. For even when we were with you, this we commanded you, If any man will not work, neither let him eat. For we hear of some that walk among you disorderly, that work not at

all, but are busybodies. Now them that are such we command and exhort in the Lord Jesus Christ, that with quietness they work, and eat their own bread." 2 Thess, iii. 7-12. There were in Thessalonica and other places in Greece, as there are now in China, idlers, busybodies or disorderly persons, who would fain live without work. From such persons Paul apprehended great danger to the infant Church; and he not only denounced them in unsparing terms, but determined by his own example to furnish a precedent which would have more weight in establishing a fixed usage in the Church than anything he could say. In addressing the Ephesian elders he gives the same reason for the course adopted. "Ye yourselves know, that these hands ministered unto my necessities, and to them that were with me. In all things I gave you an example how that so laboring ye ought to help the weak, and to remember the words of the Lord Jesus, how he himself said, It is more blessed to give than to receive." Acts xx. 34-35.

2. The Apostle in the ninth chapter of First Corinthians lays down the general rule that, as a matter of right, the teacher should depend for his temporal support on the taught; still in first introducing the Gospel to a heathen people, he felt it his duty to waive this privilege. The example which he set was that of a preacher not having his influence curtailed by the suspicion that he is laboring for pay. While the Church at home has decided that in lands where Christian institutions are established the pastor should depend for his support on his flock and abstain from secular employments, I believe it is best, at least in the first stage of mission work, for the native evangelist to follow Paul's example. Take a man laboring on the plane of his ordinary life as an earnest Christian and make him a paid laborer, and you deprive him of half his influence. It may be said that by paying him you enable him to give all his time to evangelistic work. Still it is a fair question—we are now speaking of new converts—whether a man will accomplish more for good in the end by preaching, or by simply living Christianity. The examples that we want are those of men illustrating Christianity during six days of secular work, as well as by one day of Sabbath observance. Such men and such women present Christianity in the concrete. They are "cities set on a hill," "epistles known and read of all men."

When stations multiply after this type they strike root into the soil. There is life and aggressiveness in them.

3. Some will probably ask, "Why do not missionaries themselves work with their own hands and set the same example that Paul did?" If circumstances were the same, and the course chosen by the Apostle were now practicable and would secure the same end that it did in his case, it ought to be adopted, and I believe missionaries would adopt it gladly. The reason why we do not is, that doing so in our case would defeat the object aimed at. Our circumstances as foreign missionaries in China are different from those of the Apostle Paul in almost every particular. He was a Roman citizen in the Roman empire. He labored in his native climate; was master of Greek and Hebrew, the two languages required for prosecuting his work; and his physical and intellectual training had been the same as those with whom and for whom he labored. We, in coming to China, are obliged from the first to undertake the work of acquiring a spoken and a written language, both very difficult, taxing mind and body to the utmost, and demanding all our time and energies. We have to submit to the disadvantage and drudgery of learning in comparatively advanced life—so far as we are able to do it—what the Chinaman learns, and what Paul learned, in childhood and early manhood. Besides, for a foreigner to support himself in China in competition with natives in any department of manual labor is manifestly impracticable, and one attempting to do so would diminish rather than increase his influence. Were it practicable and consistent with duty, how many of us who have a natural taste for mechanics, or agriculture, or business, would gladly spend a portion of our time in these pursuits, rather than in wearisome work of study. Is it not obvious that the only persons who can furnish in China the much needed example of propagating Christianity while they labor with their own hands, are not Europeans, but natives laboring for and among their own people?

4. The importance of trusting at first mainly to voluntary unpaid agency, or rather to the influence of Christian men and women remaining in their original callings, may be further shown by other considerations. It is a prevalent idea in China that diligent and successful attention to temporal and religious matters at the same time is impossible. We often hear the remark from Chinamen, "I am

tired of the world and its employments, and should like to enter the religion." the true interpretation of which generally is, that the man would like to avoid work and live on the "Chiao-hui." Another says, "Christianity is good, but I must earn a living for my family." Sometimes, this is a mere excuse and sometimes it expresses a man's honest conviction, that an effort to lead a Christian life will interfere with his temporal prospects. I believe that nothing is more important to the success of our work than to do away with this idea, and this can be best accomplished by living examples showing that a man may be a good Christian and a good farmer or artisan at the same time; or in other words, that "Godliness is profitable for all things, having the promise of the life that now is, and of that which is to come." Even voluntary and unpaid preaching is not to be compared for wholesome influence to earnest, consistent, Christian lives. The secret of the world's evangelization is to be found in the words of our Saviour, "So let your light shine before men, that they may see your good works, and glorify your Father which is in Heaven."

During the last few years I have often found it necessary to exhort and remonstrate with some of my people in such language as the following: "Though it is commendable for you to visit your friends and acquaintances, and to talk to them about Christianity when you have time to do so, you must not neglect your business. Your usefulness as a Christian, the religious interests of your station, and the spread of the Gospel in the neighborhood, depend largely on your success and prosperity in temporal matters. If you neglect your business and run in debt and are obliged to sell one acre of land this year and two the next, you will be a warning to all your neighbors and they will point to you and say, 'Beware of the Christian religion; our friend ____ entered it and in a few years he and his family were brought to want.' If this is the outcome of your life in temporal things, all your preaching to your neighbors will do little good."

5. Some will say that depending largely upon the voluntary and unpaid labor of native Christians for the propagation of the Gospel is pre-supposing a larger amount of zeal and devotion on their part than is found among Christians at home. If this is true, so much the worse for Christians at home. I believe the contrary, however. There is a great army of active workers at home, as well as idles. As to young converts in our country stations, it is a fact that they are willing to do

this work and able to do it, and still further that they do it. In the early history of the Church, as recorded in the Acts of the Apostles, Christianity spread chiefly through the voluntary zeal of ordinary church members, and the work of the Apostles consisted mainly in superintending and organizing the companies of Christians thus gathered. Their zeal was so great that persecution could not repress, but only intensified it. If there is not the zeal and effort in the Church at home, it is much to be deplored. Perhaps the want of it is due in a great measure to a growing habit of leaving work for Christ to be done by those who are paid for it. Where such an idea prevails, whether at home or on missionary ground, it tends to paralyze the power of the Church for good.

6. It may be objected further that this aggressive zeal to which I have referred is due largely to the expectation of being employed, and that for this reason it is not to be relied upon, since it will decline as the hope of employment diminishes. There is no doubt much truth in this. Shall we then knowingly and deliberately pander to this mercenary spirit and, by continuing to employ new converts, increase and perpetuate an evil which we deplore? or shall we not rather by refraining from employing them put a stop to the evil as soon as possible? While, however, without doubt some of these voluntary laborers are working with selfish aims, I believe there are others who work from higher and worthier motives. Let us depend on these, and we shall not be disappointed. Not giving pecuniary employment to new converts will probably retard our work for a time, at least so far as numbers of adherents is concerned, but it will promote the work in the end.

Nature of the Church and Its Development.

We may get help in learning how to deal with the new converts and stations by considering the nature of the Church and the law of its development. Christianity, whether embodied in the individual or in a Church, is the outgrowth of a vital principle. In the spiritual as well as vegetable kingdom every vital germ has its own law of life and development, and it is only by following that law that the highest development can be secured. Christianity has been introduced into the world as a plant which will thrive best confronting and contending with all the forces of its environment; not as a feeble exotic which can only live when nursed and sheltered. All unnecessary nursing will do it harm. A pine may be trained into a beautiful and fantastic shape so as to be an object of interest and curiosity, and may flourish in a way; but it will not tower heavenward as the king of the forest, unless from first to last it is subjected to the various and seemingly adverse influences of scorching sun, biting frost and raging tempest. A certain amount of care, and especially the right kind, is necessary; too much or injudicious care is injurious and may be fatal to the life which it is intended to promote.

Test Necessary before Advancement.

Young converts should be proved before they are employed and advanced to responsible public positions. It is said of deacons in the third chapter of First Timothy, "Let these also first be proved." The *also* refers no doubt to the previous qualifications required in bishops. These varied qualifications include knowledge, experience, self-culture, spiritual growth, and discipline, all combining together to form a stable and reliable basis of character. If deacons and bishops must first be proved, is there not the same necessity for proving preachers and evangelists? There are laws in civilized countries requiring that in testing an anchor-chain or a wire cable it shall be subjected to strain greater than will be required in after use before precious treasure and more precious lives are trusted to it. Ordinary prudence, aside from Scripture command, would dictate the still greater necessity of testing the character of a man who is to be used in matters affecting he temporal and spiritual interests, immediately and prospectively, of perhaps thousands. In the zeal and glow of first converts they are apt, and that unwittingly, to deceive not only us but themselves. By all means let them be proved. How can this be done without leaving them to meet the difficulties and trials incident to the condition in which they are found, and that for a considerable length of time? We have further authoritative teaching from our Saviour himself on this point, especially designed to guard against the dangers resulting from the influence of false teachers. "By their fruits ye shall know them." The outward appearance of a tree may give promise of its being everything we could desire, but we cannot be sure of its character until it bears fruit; for this we may have to wait for years, and even then find ourselves disappointed.

Necessity of Training.

Young converts before they are advanced to positions of prominence and responsibility, should also be trained.

1. The processes of proving and training, though quite different and distinct, are carried on simultaneously, and largely by the same means. This training includes not only study, but work, trial, and perhaps suffering. It should be such as will fit a man to endure hardness as a good soldier of Jesus Christ. A man may be carried through a course of theological training, freed from the struggle of ordinary life by having all his wants provided for, and yet get very little of this disciplinary training which is so important. We may think we are helping a man by relieving him of burdens when we are in fact injuring him by interfering with this training. Here again the element of time is a necessity. We are so apt to be in haste—to spur ourselves on to premature and fruitless effort by the consideration of how many souls are perishing while we are delaying. After the Apostle Paul was chosen and called, he was kept waiting nearly ten years before he was commanded to enter upon his special life work. Who will say that those ten years were not as important as any other period of his life, or that his after usefulness did not depend on them? Timothy also, by years of active and successful labor at home, obtained a good report of the brethren in Lystra and Derbe, after which he accompanied Paul as a helper; and when many years of proving and training were passed, he became Paul's co-laborer and successor in the work of evangelization and the founding of churches.

2. If it be further asked, "What then is the best way to train men for usefulness in the Church?" I know of no better answer, at least for the first stage of preparation, than to repeat the Scripture injunction, "Let every man abide in the calling wherein he was

called." Nothing else can supply the place of God's providential training in the school of ordinary life and practical experience. If God, who has called a man to the fellowship of His Church, has also called him to work of the ministry, He will manifest His purpose in His own time and way. Meanwhile, we should give these young converts all the instruction, advice, and help which Christian sympathy and prudence suggest.

Commit Converts to the Lord.

We should with faith and confidence commit young converts "to the Lord on whom they believed." This was the course unhesitatingly adopted by the Apostle Paul, and I know of no reason why we should not follow his example. Our Saviour has promised to be always with His people unto the end of the world, and to send the blessed Spirit of all grace to abide with them forever. He will give them by conferring special graces of His Spirit, prophets, teachers, exhorters, helps, and governments, as they are required. Paul on his departure from places where he had made converts often left Timothy or Silas or others to spend days or weeks in instructing, exhorting, and, comforting them, and also sent special messengers to individual churches to correct abuses and furnish help as occasion required; but we read in the Acts of the Apostles of no case in which he left any one to stay with them as their resident minister. I believe that in failing to follow this Apostolic example we have often checked the development of individual gifts, and self-reliance, and aggressive power in our Churches, making them weak, inefficient and dependent from the first.

In the meantime, in view of the great need of evangelists to enter open fields not yet reached, and of pastors and teachers to care for those who are already gathered into the fold, let us heed the solemn injunction of our Lord, "Pray ye therefore the Lord of the harvest that He send forth laborers into his harvest."

III. ORIGIN AND GROWTH OF STATIONS IN CENTRAL SHAN-TUNG

General View of the Shan-tung Work.

1. Preaching tours formed a prominent part of mission work from the first occupation of Shan-tung by Protestant missionaries in the year 1860. During the years that immediately followed, the whole eastern Shan-tung was traversed by members of the American Baptist and Presbyterian Missions. In 1866, Rev. C. W. Mateer and Rev. H. Corbett made a tour in central Shan-tung for the purpose chiefly of distributing and selling books. This was the first visit paid to Ch'ing-chou Fu and vicinity by Protestant missionaries. It was afterward visited repeatedly by Dr. Williamson and other members of the United Presbyterian Mission of Scotland, and Rev. J. MacIntyre, a member of that Mission, resided two years in Wei Hsien, the chief city of the adjacent district on the east. It was also visited from time to time by different members of the American Presbyterian mission, and in 1874 and 1875 was included in my regular itinerating tours, made twice a year.

Rev. Timothy Richard commenced regular work in Ch'ing-chou Fu as a resident missionary in 1875. There were then in that region only two converts, and these were connected with Mr. Corbett.

Previous to the work of Famine Distribution in the spring of 1877, Mr. Richard had gathered about him a little company of inquirers, and I had also a few inquirers in the district of An-ch'in, about forty-five miles. S. E. of Ch'ing-chou Fu.

2. In the spring of 1877, Mr. Richard and Rev. Alfred G. Jones gave all their time and energies to the work of Famine Relief. I took part in the same work in Kao-yai, a market town in the western extremity of An-ch'iu, and near the borders of the two other *hsien*, Lin-ch'u, and Ch'ang-lo, and continued it about three months until the close of the famine, distributing aid to about 30,000 people, from more than 300 villages.

The famine relief presented us to the people in a new and favorable light, and gave a fresh impulse to our work of evangelization. The establishment of stations may be said to have fairly begun after the famine, though a spirit of inquiry had been awakened before. In the spring of 1879, Mr. Corbett again visited this region and from this time took part in mission work there.

3. On the main points of mission policy we are happily nearly of one mind. All these stations provide their own houses of worship; none of them are cared for by a resident paid preacher; but in each of them one or more of its own members voluntarily conducts services on Sunday, and attends to the general spiritual interests of the little company of believers with whom he is connected, under the superintendence of the foreign missionary in charge. In all these stations great prominence is given to catechetical teaching and also to affording special instruction to the leaders, with a view to their teaching others. These form the distinguishing features of our work, and our main points of agreement.

4. The Baptist stations have multiplied chiefly through the voluntary labors of unpaid Christians, and radiate from the centre at Ch'ing-chou Fu. Their staff of Chinese laborers now consists of a native pastor, who is a Nanking man baptized more than twenty years ago, four evangelists paid by the mission, and two elders paid by the native Christians.

My work spread from the centre at Kao-yai, almost entirely, so far as natives are concerned, through the voluntary labors of the Chinese Christians. My staff of paid laborers at present consists of two native helpers, supported hitherto partly by the natives and partly by myself. I have from the first used a few others occasionally.

Mr. Corbett commenced his work with the assistance of church members from older stations. He has used a much larger number of helpers, and his stations are more disconnected, being found in different districts to which his preachers and evangelists have been sent. His staff of native laborers consists of about twenty-two paid helpers, and twenty teachers. The latter receive from him on an average about fifteen dollars a year, with that they can get in addition from the natives.

5. With these general statements respecting the whole field, I propose to give a more detailed account of my own stations and work, with which I am naturally more intimately acquainted. I presume, however, that in detailing my own experience I shall be giving in the main that also of my brethren. When important points of difference occur they will be spoken of *in loco*.

Relations of the Missionary Helpers and Leaders.

The characteristic feature of our stations is that the principal care of them is entrusted, not to paid preachers set over them and resident among them, but to leaders belonging to the stations. These leaders are simply church members among church members, pursuing their daily calling as before conversion. They form a very important link in the chain of influences starting from the foreign missionary. Next to the missionary is the native helper, who is generally a well-instructed Christian of some years' experience. He is under the control and direction of the missionary, and acts for him supplementing his labors and carrying out his instructions. Next to the helper is the leader, through whom principally the helper brings his influence to bear on the Christians and inquirers generally.

Principle Underlying Station Organization.

1. It is our aim that each man, woman, and child shall be both a learner from some one more advanced, and a teacher of some one less advanced. Theoretically, the missionary does nothing which the helper can do for him, the helper does nothing which the leader can do, and the leader does nothing which he can devolve upon those under him. In this way much time is saved, the gifts of all are

utilized and developed, and the station as an organized whole grows in knowledge, strength and efficiency. The leader constantly superintends, directs, and examines those under him; the helper directs and examines the leaders and their stations; and the missionary in charge has a general supervision and control of the whole.

2. It has been my habit to visit the stations regularly twice a year in order to examine carefully into the circumstances of each one of them and the progress in knowledge and performance of Christian duties of each Christian and inquirer. One of my helpers has the charge of nearly forty stations, located in four different districts or *hsien*, which he visits regularly once every two months. The other helper has the charge of about ten stations and devotes part of his time to evangelistic work outside of them. A few are without the care of a native helper, and are only visited by the foreign missionary.

3. The forty stations under one helper are divided into seven geographical groups of from four to seven stations each. The helper visits these groups in regular rotation once every two months by appointment, spending about a week in each. On Sunday he holds a general or union service, leaders and other prominent church members being present. The object aimed at is to make this union service conducted by the helper the model for the leaders to pattern after in their several stations during the seven or eight weeks when they are by themselves. Once in two months when the helper is absent, each of these groups has a similar union service conducted by the leaders, exercises and persons in charge having been appointed by the helper in advance.

4. The form of exercise for Sundays, both morning and afternoon, consists of four parts. First, a kind of informal Sunday-school in which every person present is expected, with the superintendence of the leader and those under him, to prosecute his individual studies, whether learning the Chinese character, committing to memory passages of Scripture, telling Scripture stories, or studying the catechism or Scripture question books. Second, we have the more formal service of worship, consisting of singing, reading of the Scriptures with a few explanations or exhortations, and prayer, the whole occupying not more than three quarters of an hour. Third, we have the Scripture story exercise.

Some one previously appointed tells the story; the leader of the meeting then calls on different persons one after another to reproduce it in consecutive parts, and afterward all present take part in drawing practical lessons and duties from it. There is never a time for more than one story, and often that one has to be divided and has two Sundays given to it. Fourth, if there is time a catechetical exercise follows in which all unite, designated to bring out more clearly the meaning of what they have already learned—as the Lord's Prayer, the Ten Commandments, select passages of Scripture, some book of Scripture, or some special subject such as the duty of benevolence, etc. This general order of exercises is modified or varied when the circumstances of a station make it advisable that it should be.

5. Leaders are sometimes formally selected by their stations. More generally, however, they find themselves in this position as the natural result of providential circumstances. In many cases the leader is the person who originated the station with which he is connected, the other members having been brought into the Church by his instrumentality. These members look up to him as their natural head and teacher, and a strong feeling of gratitude, Christian sympathy, and responsibility grows up spontaneously. In some cases persons brought in afterward are more gifted or literary than the original leader and after a time take his place, or are associated with him as joint leaders. In some stations women are the first converts, and even after men have joined them, exert a marked if not the chief influence, and take a prominent part in teaching, exhortation, and prayer.

6. The chapels, with the chapel furniture, are provided by the natives themselves. As a rule they are not separate buildings, but form a part of the ordinary Chinese dwelling house. Often the chapel belongs to the leader. Sometimes it is rented by the Christians, and in a few places it is a new building specially erected for the purpose of worship. When this is the case, Christians from other villages assist with their contributions, and I have also generally contributed, to the amount of about one-tenth of the value of the building. The cost of these chapels ranges from thirty to one hundred dollars each. There is as yet no chapel the ownership of which is vested in the Church as a whole. Even when a new building is erected, it belongs to the man on whose ground it stands. The fact that the chapels form a part of

the ordinary dwellings houses of the people exempts the Christians, I think, from a good deal of prejudice and persecution which is apt to be excited by and directed toward distinctive church buildings.

Instruction of Inquirers and Church Members.

Perhaps the most important question which can arise in connection with our country stations is, How shall we most effectually carry out the command of our Savior, "Feed my sheep," "Feed my lambs."

1. As has been before indicated, the persons mainly depended upon for performing this work are the leaders. In our present circumstances in Shan-tung, no other plan is possible. Where could we obtain native preachers for teaching and superintending the one hundred and fifty stations already established? There are less than a dozen candidates for the ministry in the whole field. We cannot yet know how many of these will be acceptable to the people, and the number of stations is constantly increasing. Were it desirable to supply each station with a native preacher we have not the men, and it would not be reasonable to suppose that we should have at this stage of our work. If we had the men, who would support them? 'The natives at present are too weak to do it, and if the foreign Boards were able to assume this burden, their doing so would establish a precedent which would add very much to the difficulties of making the native churches independent and self-supporting in the future.

2. In my opinion we may go a step farther, and say that the introduction of paid teachers in each station, even if it were possible, would not at present be desirable. The leaders understand better than a person from a distance could, the individual peculiarities of the neighbors, and also the tones and inflections of the local dialect, local expressions, illustrations, and habits of thought. They are likely to be more interested in those about them, most of whom may be called their own converts, than any one else could be, and are more disposed to give them the care and attention necessary in instructing beginners. In teaching they set an example to others, a larger number of teachers is thus secured than could be obtained in any other way,

and learning and teaching go on together, the one preparing for the other, and the teaching being an important part of the learning, perhaps quite as useful to the teacher as to the taught. Though the knowledge of the leaders may be elementary and incomplete, they are quite in advance of the other church members and inquirers, and what they do know is just what the others need first to learn. The leaders are especially fitted to communicate this knowledge, simply because they are not widely separated in intelligence and sympathy from those who are to be taught.

3. It must be admitted that in this matter of appointing leaders we meet in the beginning with serious difficulties. Sometimes it is almost impossible to find one. The station contains perhaps not a single person who can read. Even then, however, a modification of our plan is found to work good results in the end. If the weak station is within reach of a stronger, older one, it can obtain help by worshipping with and gaining instruction from it, or by some member of the older station coming to spend Sunday with his less advanced and less favored brethren. The helper, too, is expected to give special time and care to these weak stations. There are not a few cases of men, and also of women, who at first could not read, who can now read the Scriptures, teach and lead the singing, and are not only efficient leaders in their own stations but exert a happy influence outside of it.

4. From the first, we emphasize teaching rather than preaching. I here use the word "preaching" in its specific sense of logical and more or less elaborate dissertation. We should remember that continuous discourse is something which is almost unknown in China. Even educated Chinamen follow it with difficulty. A carefully prepared sermon from a trained native preacher or a foreign missionary, such a sermon as would be admirably suited to an intelligent educated Christian congregation, is out of place in a new station. From the fact that it is adapted to another kind of congregation, it is by necessary consequence unsuitable here. An attempt at formal preaching by those who have neither the Scriptural knowledge nor the intellectual and practical training to fit them for it is still more to be deprecated. We who are accustomed from childhood to instruction by lectures and sermons, naturally and very properly introduce them in the mission centres where we are located;

and our personal teachers and pupils trained in our schools become accustomed to them and are profited by them. In the country stations a few of the more advanced Christians may be benefited by a sermon, but to the great body of hearers who most need instruction it would be like listening to utterances in an unknown tongue. This kind of preaching gives rise in the Church from its very infancy to a kind of formalism which is almost fatal to growth and progress. The congregation rises, or sits, or kneels as directed, and may maintain a reverent attitude and listen, or have the appearance of listening, to what is said: in a word they have a service and go home with their consciences satisfied, but their minds not enlightened. Even the Quaker method of sitting before God in silent meditation or mute reverence would be preferable to having the mind distracted by allusions to something they have not heard of, thoughts beyond their reach and processes of reasoning which they cannot follow. I am far from saying that no good is accomplished. Those who engage in such a service, as many of them do, feeling that they are offering homage and worship to the true God their Heavenly Father, though they may only catch an occasional idea from a prayer, or an exhortation, or a sermon, will be benefited, and their worship will no doubt be accepted. Most of the persons in our congregations are, as regards their mental development, in the condition of children and have to be treated as such.

5. But to return to the methods of teaching which we have been led to adopt. All converts at first receive more or less oral instruction and direction from the foreign missionary, or the native helper, or the leader by whom they are brought into the Church. They are required to commit to memory and to learn the meaning of a simple catechism containing a compendium of Christian doctrine, and also forms of prayer and passages of Scripture. During the period of probation they are expected to attend services regularly and to perform the religious duties of professing Christians. The time of probation has varied from six months — or less in exceptional cases — to one or two years. Our English Baptist brethren have recently increased it, fixing the minimum at eighteen months.

We have found it necessary, in order to systematize and unify our work, to establish rules and regulations, which have been put up in the chapels as placards. Most of these, having been adopted by Mr.

Corbett and myself, are now embodied in the new edition of the "Manual for Inquirers," which is published by the North China Tract Society. This Manual, the Catechism and the Gospels, are the books which I place in the hands of every inquirer, and little more is needed for years in the way of text-books for those who have not previously learned to read.

The Manual contains, —General Directions for Prosecuting Scripture Studies; Forms of Prayer; the Apostles' Creed; and Select Passages of Scripture—to be committed to memory. Then follows a large selection of Scripture stories and parables, with directions as to how they should be recited and explained; only the titles of these are given with references to the place in the Bible where they are to be found. Next follow: Rules for the Organization and Direction of Stations; Duties of Leaders and Rules for their Guidance; a system of forms for keeping Station Records of attendance and studies, etc.; Form of Church Covenant; Scripture Lessons for Preparing for Baptism; the same for preparing for the Lord's Supper; Order of Exercises for Church Service and Directions for Spending Sunday; a short Scripture Catechism—enforcing the duty of giving of our substance for benevolent purposes; and a short essay on the Duty of Every Christian to make known the Gospel to Others. To the whole is appended questions on the various parts, specially prepared to facilitate the teaching and examination of learners. A selection of our most common Hymns is also sometimes bound up with the volume.

6. Studies prosecuted are divided into six kinds. All church members and inquirers are supposed to be carrying on two or three of these at the same time, of which a complete record is kept. The six kinds of studies are—learning to read, memorizing Scripture, reading Scripture in course, telling Scripture stories, learning the meaning of Scripture, and reviews of former exercises. The books used are almost exclusively in Mandarin, in the Chinese character.

7. We find Catechisms and Scripture question books of great use, not only for inquirers, but for the more advanced Christians. I give great prominence to learning and reciting Scripture stories and parables, and nothing has been found to produce more satisfactory results. It excites interest, develops thought, and furnishes in a simple form a compendium of Bible history and Christian duty; while a careful training in relating Bible Stories and drawing

practical lessons from them is one of the best ways of developing preaching talent wherever it is found.

8. Scholars as well as the illiterate are required to learn the Manual, not only for their own sakes, but in order to teach others. They soon familiarize themselves with its contents, and pass on to the general study of the Scriptures with the help of commentaries.

Bible or Training Classes.

The stations of Mr. Corbett and myself are on an average about two hundred miles distant from our home in Chefoo. In visiting them we have only time for necessary examinations, together with general instructions and directions. To secure thorough and methodical teaching, no plan has been found practicable but that of a select number of the learners coming to us in Chefoo. These have been organized into classes which have formed a kind of Normal School. At first inquirers came. Since stations have been established, inquirers in the vicinity of them prepare for baptism at home.

1. For several years past our classes have been composed of the more advanced church members especially selected and invited. They come with the understanding that in going back to their homes they are to communicate what they have learned to others. They are in no sense in our employ or pay, and their previous occupations and relations continue as before. As we are absent on our tours in the spring and autumn, the classes assemble in Chefoo during the summer and winter months when we are at home and continue in session from six weeks to two months.

2. In many cases we have been obliged to pay the travelling expenses of members of the classes in returning home, the money they bring with them being as a rule expended before the session is over. During the last few years, however, not a few have provided their own travelling expenses for both coming and returning. During their stay with us they are our guests, we furnishing them with food and lodgings. We have found this course necessary and do not think it under the circumstances unreasonable. Most of these students are poor and could not afford to pay all their expenses. Coming as they do requires what is to them a considerable outlay in providing decent

clothing and food by the way. The loss of time in attending the class is also to some a matter of no small importance. Many incur heavy expenses in the course of the year in discharging the duties of Christian hospitality in their homes, where they have frequent visits from natives and foreigners; so that in entertaining them while with us, we are only in part repaying in kind what they have already expended in establishing and extending the work in their own neighborhoods.

3. The studies while with us are mainly Scriptural, with additional elementary instruction in astronomy, geography, history, and general knowledge. Here, as in the stations, lessons are carried on catechetically, and what is taught one day is the subject of examination the next. Much attention is also given to rehearsing Scripture stories. One hour a day is assigned to instruction in vocal music, which has been taught for many years, principally by Mrs. Nevius, who has devoted herself to it with singular assiduity and success. While the classes are with us we give nearly all our time and strength to them. Those who come here with an earnest purpose to learn, enjoy the exercises and are benefited by them; those who do not, cannot bear the pressure and soon find an excuse for going home.

My classes have numbered of late about forty. So far as practicable, the same individuals come year after year. They have gone over the Gospels—some of them repeatedly—the Acts of the Apostles, Romans and several of the other Epistles, and parts of the Old Testament. Their proficiency in Scripture knowledge will compare favorably with that that of intelligent adult classes in Sunday-schools at home. They could sustain a very creditable examination on the Acts of the Apostles, and also on Romans, mastering the argument and being able to reproduce it. Some have written while here so full and clear an analysis of that Epistle that their manuscripts were sought for and copied by others who could not come to the class. The hymns which they sing are for the most part translations of familiar English hymns, in the same meters as the originals, and sung to the same familiar tunes. They are taught to sing by note and some of them read music very well. They have great difficulty with the half tones, their scale and ours being different

4. These classes have almost fulfilled their purpose and will probably soon give place to theological classes, those who have attended them having acquired such a familiarity with the Scriptures as enables them now to carry on their studies at home, with the help of commentaries and other Christian books.

Results to Station Members.

The proficiency in Christian knowledge of the members of these country stations will, I think, bear favorable comparison with that of the converts cared for by resident preachers.

1. The degree of illiteracy of the inhabitants of these rural districts is perhaps somewhat greater than that of the population of China taken as a whole. Not more than one out of twenty of the men can read, and not one of a thousand of the women. Among our Christians, nearly all the children and most of the adults of both sexes under fifty years of age learn to read. Some have made remarkable progress in the study of the Scriptures. A large proportion of them have committed to memory the Sermon on the Mount and many other select passages of the Bible. Scripture ideas and phrases have entered into the language of everyday life. Persons of advanced age, though themselves unable to read, take great pleasure in relating Scripture stories and parables, and in teaching others less instructed what they have learned.

2. The mental development of the converts and their enthusiasm in their studies have in many places attracted the attention and excited the wonder of their heathen neighbors. In one of our stations there is a literary man named Fu, now over fifty years of age, who has been totally blind for more than twenty years. He has taught his daughter, a girl of fifteen, to read the Bible, she describing the characters as seen, and he telling her the names and meanings of them. She has in this way learned about two thousand characters. Her father has memorized from her lips the gospels of Matthew and John, the Acts of the Apostles, and Romans, and many other portions of Scripture. He and other members of his family have taught his sister, Mrs. Kung, who is also blind, to repeat nine chapters of Matthew, and this blind woman has taught her invalid, bedridden

sister-in-law, Mrs. Wang, to read the scriptures, by repeating them to her character by character from memory, while her sister-in-law finds out the words on the printed page.

Manner in which Stations are Propagated.

Many of the stations in this province originated, as before stated, in the labors of paid agents employed as evangelists. When new ones are established, however, they are usually organized under a leader chosen on the plan detailed above. The English Baptist stations and my own have for the most part been established without the help of paid evangelists. They radiate from self-propagating centres, reminding one of sarmentaceous plants which propagate themselves by runners striking root and producing new plants in their vicinity of the parent stock, the new plants in their turn repeating the same process.

1. When a man becomes a Christian the fact is known through the whole circle of his acquaintances, male and female, far and wide. It is generally believed that his mind has lost its balance. He is shunned for a time, but before long his friends visit him either from sympathy or curiosity. They find him in apparently a normal condition and working quietly in his shop or on his farm, and are curious to know what this new departure means. An opportunity is thus afforded of presenting the claims of Christianity as not the religion of the foreigner but the true religion for all mankind. The visitor goes home and thinks about the matter and comes again, attends service on Sunday, is interested in the truth, makes a profession of Christianity, and in process of time his home becomes new propagating centre. Stations started in this manner have the advantage of a natural connection with the parent station, and they are nourished and supported by it until they are strong enough to have the connection severed and live and grow independently.

2. The Baptist mission, having tried both methods for some years past in the same field, have found that as a rule the stations which have originated as the result of the labors of paid agents have been comparatively weak and unreliable, and some have entirely fallen away, while those which have been commenced on the self-

propagating principle have generally maintained a healthy, vigorous growth. Instead of increasing their paid agents as the number of church members has increased, that mission has diminished them nearly one-half. This self-propagating principle often results in the establishment of stations one or two days' journey from the propagating centre.

3. I have often been asked, "Why do you not employ and pay more native agents?" I reply by another question, Why should I? The only men I could employ are exerting what influence they have for good where they now are. My paying them money and transferring them from one place to another would not make them better men nor increase their influence. It might have the opposite effect. During the last few years I have in fact frequently been inclined to attempt to enlarge and hasten on the work by selecting and employing native agents from my stations, and have requested money appropriations from our society to enable me to do so. When the time has come for carrying out this plan, however, I have refrained from taking the proposed step, fearing that it would do more harm than good.

4. I am asked again, "Do you intend never to employ native paid agents?" My reply is, I leave this question to be determined by the circumstances and in the light of the future. If suitable men are found and it is clear that employing them as paid agents would do good, I should be glad to see them employed, and the more of them the better.

Classes to which Our Church Members Belong.

Most of our stations are found in country villages, and in general the Christians may be said to belong to the middle class. Although none of them are what we should call rich, not a few are "well-to-do" as compared to the majority of their own people. Many are farmers and day laborers. We have also school-teachers, artisans, peddlers, and innkeepers. As a rule men preponderate in numbers, though some churches are composed mostly of women. Sometimes the men are first reached and influence the women of their families to follow them, and sometimes the reverse is the case. The work among the women has in my stations, and in the main in all the others, been carried on without the help of foreign ladies. A few country women have come to Chefoo to receive instruction from Mrs. Nevius. In most places visits of ladies, except the wives of missionaries accompanying their husbands, would hitherto have been impracticable and, in the opinion of the native Christians, undesirable. The common assertion that heathen women cannot be evangelized through the instrumentality of men is certainly not universally true in China. Facts prove the contrary. In most places, indeed generally in the interior at a distance from the established central stations, they can hardly be reached and evangelized except by men. In many of the Shan-tung stations women stand out prominently as examples of zeal and proficiency in Christian knowledge.

Persecution.

1. Opposition and persecution have marked the course of our work to a greater or less extent in every district. The authority of the family or clan is often invoked to overrule the individual in his determination to enter the new religion. Village elders and trustees of temples unite in efforts to exact from Christians contributions for theatres and the repairs of temples. When native Christians persist in asserting their purpose to follow their own convictions of duty in opposition to those who think they have both the right and the power to control them, open outbreaks ensue, resulting in brutal assaults, houseburning and in some cases driving Christians from their homes. Native Christians are sometimes arraigned before the local magistrates on fictitious charges; and when it is found, as at times is the case, that the local magistrate is only too glad to join in the persecution, false accusations become more numerous, and old law-suits in which the Christians were parties are revived. In these litigations the persecutors have every advantage. There are among them those familiar with all the arts and intricacies of Chinese law-suits, and those who have friends in the *ya-mên* and money for bribery when it is required. Under these circumstances the Christians have small hope of justice. Charges are brought against them with such a show of plausibility, and such an array of evidence, that

officers who are disposed to act justly, as I believe some of them are, may almost be excused for regarding Christians as guilty culprits and treating them accordingly.

2. In cases of great injustice and abuse, missionaries have taken up the complaints of the native Christians, appealed to their consuls, and in some instances obtained partial redress. It must be acknowledged, however, that we have not invariably elicited correct representations of these cases; and also that, when through the influence of the foreign teachers the tide of fortune has turned in favor of the Christians, they have not always been free from a spirit of revenge and retaliation. Bitter and unjust as the treatment has been which our Christians have often received, it is a growing opinion here that the best weapons with which to meet this opposition are Christian patience and forebearance, and that the surest victory and the one which will be followed by the best results is that of "overcoming evil with good." We are less disposed to appeal to the civil power on behalf of our people, except in extreme cases.

Sabbath Observance.

1. The difficulty of enforcing strict rules of Sabbath observance is not less here than in other parts of China. Our own mission has taken strong ground on this subject. We regard the Sabbath, not as a Jewish institution, but an institution for man in all ages wherever found. We believe it has the same authority as the other commandments of the decalogue; that the obligation to keep one day holy unto the Lord antedates the decalogue, as the duties enjoined in the other commandments do; and that the decalogue is but the divine reannunciation and publication of universal and eternal law. As such we hold that it can never be abrogated, that its observance is inseparably connected with the prosperity of the Church, and an index of its spiritual state.

2. In determining how Sunday shall be observed, or in other words, in the interpretation of the fourth commandment, we have an infallible guide in the teachings of our Saviour. He has declared that it is lawful and right (1) to do good on the Sabbath day; (2) to perform acts of necessity; (3) of mercy and kindness; (4) to perform

work connected with or necessary to the worship and service of God; (5) that, as the Sabbath was made for man and not man for the Sabbath, this commandment should be so construed as to subserve and not interfere with man's best and highest good. God's revelation of truth and duty is one consistent whole, each part connected with and conditioned by the others. Cases may occur in which one command overrules and supersedes another. The paramount authority and command of God make it a man's duty under some circumstances to disobey a parent; the civil law or the inherent right to preserve one's own life against lawless violence, may make it right to destroy human life; and the necessities of war or famine may justify a man in taking and using what does not belong to him. So circumstances may justify the performance of ordinary labor on the Sabbath, in which case such labor is not to be regarded as ignoring or breaking the fourth commandment, but as obeying God's will in the exceptional as well as the usual observance of the day. Nothing should be done which the above principles laid down by our Saviour do not warrant.

3. It is evident that the natural outcome of these principles must be a great diversity of practice, growing out of varied situations and conditions. It is evident also that the application of these principles must be left largely to each individual Christian. I believe this may safely be done so long as the divine obligation of the command is acknowledged. On the graduated scale, representing on one hand actions plainly inadmissible, and on the other, actions as manifestly admissible, there is a wide medium of debatable ground where room must be left for the exercise of individual liberty and Christian charity. To make the matter more practical. On the side of unjustifiable Sunday labor we may designate that of the farmer who tills his own land and is, or ought to be, the master of his own establishment; or the artisan who works in his own shop with or without employees. In such cases as these we insist on a strict observance of the Sabbath and make a breach of this observance a matter of censure and discipline. On the side of justifiable work we designate enforced labor performed on Sunday by slaves, minors, daughters-in-law etc. In our stations the duty of Sabbath observance is generally acknowledged, and I think I may say that there is a manifest improvement in public sentiment on this subject. In my

own field there is a considerable proportion of the stations in which the observance of the day is gratifying and commendable; but in majority of these stations strict observance is the exception, and a loose and partial one the rule. We hope to see a gradual advancement in this matter as the result, with God's grace and help, of careful Bible teaching and the examples of our more advanced and conscientious Christians.

4. It may be objected that insisting on the divine obligation of Sabbath observance, and at the same time providing for the relaxing or annulling of these obligations, practically leads to about the same result as leaving the whole matter to be determined by individual choice or expediency. It should be remembered, however, that this modification or relaxation is not one of our suggestion, but is specifically laid down by the Lord of the Sabbath Himself. The practice here advocated provides, too, for the gradual and finally complete introduction of the Sabbath into heathen lands on a basis of divine authority; while the theory that the Sabbath was only a Jewish institution makes the observance of it a matter of choice rather than duty, and condones for its neglect or abuse, which gradually becomes a habit interwoven with social and national customs. Under one theory, so far as this question is concerned, the Church is like a ship at turn of tide drifting in different directions in obedience to the temporary influences of wind and tide, but still holding fast to her anchor and destined to settle soon in a fixed position; under the other theory she is without anchor and drifting hopelessly.

Discipline.

1. We regard the administrations of discipline as indispensable to the growth and prosperity of our work, and attention to it claims a large portion of our time and thoughts. With the use of our Record Book, the assistance of our leaders and helpers and information obtained from other sources, the difficulty in gaining a knowledge of the real state of things is not so great as might at first be supposed.

2. The proportion of those who have been excommunicated on account of scandalous offences is comparatively small. The great majority of them, perhaps as many as eighty per cent, are cases of gradual and at last complete neglect of Christian duties, commencing

with giving up Bible study, disregard of the Sabbath and neglect of public worship. It now appears that most of these persons entered the Church without a clear apprehension of what Christianity, theoretical and practical, is. Their motives seem to have been to obtain a place as a preacher or servant, or pecuniary aid in other ways, or to get help in law-suits, actual or anticipated—all these motives being connected no doubt with the sincere conviction that Christianity is true and a desire to share in the spiritual blessings which it confers. They were also ignorant of the difficulties and trials connected with a Christian profession, and so when they met with opposition and persecution they fell away.

3. We administer discipline as directed by the Scriptures and generally practiced by Christian churches at home: first, by exhortation and admonition, followed if necessary by a formal trial and suspension; and after a period of suspension varying from few months to one or two years, in failure of reformation, by excommunication.

4. The whole number of adult baptisms in my own field during the last seven years has been about one thousand. The proportion of excommunicated persons is about twenty per cent of the whole, and more than half of them have been from the one *hsien*, Shiu-kuang, where there were for a time numerous accessions under a good deal of excitement. In the other four *hsien*, the proportion of excommunicated persons as compared to the whole number of converts is about ten per cent. While there has been this falling away in individuals, there has been a comparatively slight loss of stations, nearly all having left in them a few earnest men; so that the places where there have been most excommunications are really stronger and more promising than when they had more names on the roll. No station has as yet been entirely given up. It is feared, however, that we shall soon have to give up four, three of them in the district of Shiu-kuang.

5. Cases of discipline have diminished considerably during the last year, and we hope the number may be much curtailed in the future by avoiding some of the causes which have led to them. Very few excommunicated persons have returned to us. Very few have become enemies and open opposers. Most are indifferent, some soured and disappointed. Many of them retain strong sympathy with

the Church and continue to attend services. In every case, so far as I know, the administration of discipline has been sustained by public opinion in the Church and outside of it, and the effect of discipline has been decidedly good. I believe the neglect of it would soon result in checking the growth and perhaps extinguishing the life of the Church.

6. It has been objected to this plan of conducting stations that with the missionary living so far away from them, and the new converts left so much to themselves, it is impossible for him to know what is occurring, and the difficulties of finding out and correcting abuses and irregularities must be greatly increased. There is weight in this objection; but, in my opinion, the difficulties are much less than might be imagined and the advantages of the stations being left to themselves far outweigh the disadvantages. The helper is able to find out quite as much about the stations as the missionary could if he were constantly living among them. While there may be motives at work influencing church members to conceal important facts from the missionary and also from the helper, there are other motives which work strongly in the opposite direction. Irregularities or improprieties on the part of an individual or party in the Church are very likely to be reported on the first opportunity by another individual or party. Should a whole station be interested in concealing something which ought to be known, some adjoining station, or people outside the Church, will probably be found ready to give the requisite information. Our main dependence, however, is on the honesty and integrity of the leaders and the church members, especially on the fact that the station is theirs and not the missionary's, and that they, rather than he, are the ones who are chiefly interested in correcting abuses. The fact that they do not depend upon the missionary for pecuniary support, which eliminates the strongest motive for concealment or deception, is a matter of much greater importance than the proximity or distance of the missionary. Many facts will prove that where there is a motive to deceive, the daily presence and supervision of the missionary is no sure guarantee against concealment and deception being carried on during a long course of years.

Contributions.

In contributions we have not accomplished what we ought. This matter has been constantly kept before the Christians, and special books and placards treating of this subject have been prepared for them and studied by them. A good beginning has been made in ways which it is not easy to tabulate and publish in public reports. Chapels have been built and furnished; a good deal has been done especially by those who are connected with chapels in entertaining and instructing inquirers; voluntary labor in evangelizing the "regions beyond" has been carried on to a considerable extent; and poor church members have been assisted. In addition to this, most of the stations have given a contribution through the foreign missionary once or twice a year, varying in amount from one to three or four dollars or more, which has been applied hitherto to paying the expenses of the helpers. Our Christians need further instruction as to the duty of giving and more pressure to induce them to give, and also to have placed before them objects suited to draw out their sympathies. The example of other missions has been very helpful to us.

Schools.

The opinions and policy of the missionaries here as to schools vary considerably, and the course to be taken in the future is not yet fixed. There are but few places where the native Christians are strong enough in numbers and wealth to support schools of their own. One member of our mission is trying the experiment of helping country day schools, paying about one dollar a year for each pupil. This help is furnished on the conditions that the schools have Christian teachers, that the pupils learn Christian books, and are subject to the examination and control of the foreign missionary and his helper. A similar plan has been adopted to some extent by the English Baptist missionaries.

For myself I have not been successful with this plan. I am helping three day schools this year to the amount of from five to eight dollars to each school. These are started by the natives who applied to me for assistance. In each of them, I am disposed to think that a prominent, if not the chief motive, is to provide a support for the teacher, who otherwise would have no source of income.

So far no plan for schools has seemed to me so practicable and satisfactory in its results as that of making stations themselves a kind of training school for all their members. A great deal may be accomplished by systematic teaching on Sunday and also employing leisure months and days in study.

The plan of free day school during the winter months, when the farmers have little to do, suggested and adopted last winter in one of the stations, has interested me greatly and I should like very much to see it or something similar generally adopted.

Men Employed and Incidental Expenses.

1. From the more than eight hundred church members in my stations, I have at present in my own employ two men, viz., one helper, who receives five thousand cash ($4.67) per month, and one servant. The other helper is from one of the older stations. Besides these, there are the following men from my stations in the employ of other missionaries, viz., two teachers, three helpers, and six servants, making the whole number employed and paid by foreigners thirteen.

2. Besides these, I have for several years supported from private funds a young man from a wealthy family who has been driven from his home by violent and continued persecution. His expenses are from fifty to seventy dollars a year. He is now studying medicine and doing a good medical and evangelistic work in and about his home. He will, I hope, soon be independent and require no further help.

3. The amount expended for providing food for the Bible classes at Chefoo composed of leaders from the stations has been about one hundred dollars a year. By tabulating the above and other items we have the following as the entire expense for my stations for the past year, 1885, aside from the salary and itinerating expenses of the foreign missionary:

Salary of two helpers.................................	$112.00
Aid to one medical student...........................	65.00
Bible classes...	54.00
Contributions to three day schools....................	18.00
Contributions towards building chapels............	14.60
Occasional preaching tours...........................	15.80
Help in cases of persecution...........................	19.18
Total...	298.58

About one-half of this sum total is supplied by the mission. The above will present a fair average of expenses and the number of men employed from year to year. It does not include private assistance given to the poor, amounting during the past year to about forty dollars. In 1884 I had an additional helper, and in 1883 two additional ones—both from the college at Têng-chou Fu. I expect to have for the coming year, 1886, but one paid helper.

Summary and Forecast.

The foregoing statements will give, I think, a correct general idea of the character and condition of these stations at present. They are marked by the same weaknesses and defects which are found in a greater or less degree in churches everywhere, and which we should expect to find in converts just emerging from the darkness of heathenism who are still surrounded by heathen influences and only imperfectly emancipated from old heathen habits. In every respect they fall short of the Christian ideal and the ideal of the plan on which we are working. I am glad to be able to say, however, that the evidences of vitality and growth are more and more apparent every year; that individual Christians are advancing in knowledge and spirituality; that the stations are in the main giving evidence of stability and promise of permanency; and that they are gaining a good report from those who are without.

What the future of these stations will be we cannot know. In view of the dangers to which they are exposed and the disappointing results which have so often marked the history of missionary enterprises in China, we can only "rejoice with trembling." Our hope is in the continued presence and blessing of our Divine Master. We rejoice that this vine of God's planting is striking its roots into the native soil, and we believe that with God's blessing it will continue to grow and spread wide its branches and bring forth fruit to His glory.

IV. ORGANIZATION OF STATIONS, PRESENT AND PROSPECTIVE

Varying Views Concerning Church Organization.

1. The question, What is the best mode of organization for native converts in new stations? scarcely enters the mind on one's first arrival in China. Most of us are satisfied that the mode adopted by that branch of the Church with which we are severally connected is the best; that it is, if not the one specially enjoined by Scripture authority, at least the one most in harmony with Scripture teachings, and fully sanctioned by practical experience. Moreover, it is the one with the working of which we are individually most familiar and into the practice of which we naturally and unquestioningly fall. If we are unable to adopt it at once, it is a matter of regret and we are anxious to put it into operation as soon as possible.

2. When the missionary, associated with co-laborers of different nationalities and church connections, looks at the question of organization from the stand-point of mission work on heathen ground, it assumes new aspects, and a few years experience and observation will probably effect a considerable modification of views. He soon finds that missionaries of different denominations ignore in a measure for the time being their several systems and, in the first stage of their work, agree in the main in a new plan which all have adopted under the force of circumstances. He sees companies of Christians placed under the care of unofficial religious teachers, and native evangelists preaching in unevangelized districts, while there are as yet no organized churches, and perhaps no bishops, elders, or deacons, nor even candidates for the ministry;— only missionaries, and native preachers having the names of "helpers," "catechists," "native assistants," *"colporteurs,"* "Bible

agents," or "evangelists." In places where stations have reached a more advanced stage of development, requiring some sort of organization, missionaries are sometimes led by personal proclivities and local circumstances to the adoption of methods quite aside from their previous antecedents. Not long since in a conference at Chefoo of missionaries from different parts of China, it was discovered that an Independent was carrying on his work on Presbyterian principles, "because they suited best in this field;" in the methods of another Independent from a different province the prelatical element predominated, while a Presbyterian was found working on a plan which had a very little of Presbyterianism in it, but a singular blending of Methodism, Independency, and Prelacy.

3. What lessons are we to learn from these facts? Is it not this, that practical experience seems to point to the conclusion that present forms of church organization in the West are not to be, at least without some modification, our guides in the founding of infant churches in a heathen land? If it be asked, What then is to be our guide? I answer, The teachings of the New Testament. If it be further asked, Are we to infer, then, that all the forms of church organization in the West are at variance with Scripture teaching? I answer, By no means. A plan of organization in England or America may be very different from one adopted in China, and both though different may be equally Scriptural; and one of them may be suited to the home church and one to a mission station, just because they are different.

The all-important question is, What do the Scriptures teach respecting church organization? Do they lay down a system with fixed and unvarying rules and usages, to be observed at all times and under all circumstances? Or a system based on general principles, purposely flexible and readily adapting itself, under the guidance of God's Spirit and providence and common sense, to all the conditions in which the Church can be placed? I believe the latter is the true supposition. The same conclusion might be inferred from the fact that, while the doctrines of Christianity, which are obviously and by common consent regard as fundamental and essential, are taught in the Scriptures specifically, elaborately and repeatedly, there is no portion of Scripture where a complete and detailed system of church government is presented or referred to. It may be said, and very truly, that God might reveal to us a complete and authoritative system of church government, inferentially as well as explicitly. Had he done so, however, would there not have been a general agreement with regard to these teachings as there is with regard to Christian doctrine?

I believe that the distinctive principles which underlie the different systems of church organization prevailing in the West are all Scriptural. The principle of the authority and responsibility of individual believers in matters relating to the conduct of the Church is a very prominent part of the teaching of the New Testament. The importance of appointing elders, or bishops, as authoritative leaders and rulers in the Church is taught no less clearly. The Scriptural sanction for the appointment, at least in the early history of the Church, of superintendents or overseers, having the charge and the care of many associated churches with their elders and deacons, is no less evident. The degree of prominence or proportionate use of these different principles or elements of church organization may vary indefinitely according to the condition and requirements of the church. This theory provides for constant change and modification suited to the stage of the church's development, the character of its members and its conditions and surroundings.

If I mistake not, diversity and gradual progression in the application of these principles is distinctly traceable in the New Testament. The Gospels and the earlier part of the Acts of the Apostles indicate a very simple form of organization, or no pronounced form; and the latter part of the Acts, with the Epistles, shows a more complete system gradually developed from previously established germinal principles. Constant development and change in divergent directions mark the whole course of ecclesiastical history from the Apostolic period to the present time. How far these developments have been Scriptural, or in accordance with the leadings of God's spirit, and promotive of the best interests of the Church, it does not fall within the province of these letters to inquire. May we not, however, raise the general question as to whether the present forms of church government are not severally characterized by the special development of some one element to the exclusion of others which should supplement and modify it, presenting abnormal and disproportionate growths, each Scriptural in its dominating idea, but unscriptural in its human narrowness?

4. Another question arises in this connection of great importance. In our present position of missionaries representing different branches of the Church, closely related to one another in a common work, our methods simple and presenting many points of agreement, and our different systems of organization in a rudimental undeveloped state, should we not make use of our opportunity to avoid as far as possible in the future the divergences which impair the unity and efficiency of the Church at home, retaining and perpetuating a degree of uniformity and co-operation which in western lands seems impracticable? Is it not our duty to do this? Would it not be in accordance with the express teachings of our Saviour and also with the wishes of most of those whom we represent? Would it not have a decided influence for good on the home churches?

5. On the supposition that present forms of church organization are adapted to secure the best spiritual interests of the Church in the West, the presumption is that in certain respects they are for that very reason not adapted to the wants of mission churches in China. What circumstances could differ more widely than those of churches which are the development of centuries or a millennium of Christian culture, and those just emerging from heathenism?

Scripture Teachings as to the Best System for China.

The question recurs, What may we learn from the Scriptures as to the best system of organization and supervision for the Church in China at the present time?

1. The extension of the Church must depend mainly on the godly lives and voluntary activities of its members.

In early times, as a result of ordinary business and social intercourse and the aggressive zeal of early Christians, Christianity found its way to Cyprus, Syria, Cilicia and Egypt, and as far west as Rome. The disciples went everywhere preaching the Word. A great advance had been made before the Apostle Paul was called from his home by Barnabas to assist and strengthen the disciples already gathered at Antioch. Wherever he went afterwards in his work of establishing churches in new fields, he obtained from the believers gathered into the Church numerous voluntary helpers and coadjutors, both men and women.

I can find no authority in the Scriptures, either in specific teaching or Apostolic example, for the practice so common nowadays, of seeking out and employing paid agents as preachers. At the time when Paul commenced his public ministry, the churches established in Syria and Cilicia might no doubt have furnished a large number of such persons, if they had been wanted. It may be said that there were no missionary boards at that time and that the Church was too weak to undertake such an enterprise. This explanation, however, does not meet the case. Paul did not hesitate to call upon the churches for contributions when they were needed. He evidently thought them able to give and that it was their privilege and an advantage to themselves to give, and they did contribute freely when they were asked to do so.

The evils resulting from employing new converts as paid agents for preaching the Gospel have been referred to in previous pages. What we wish to emphasize here is that such a course is without precedent in the Bible. The members of the early Church were all witness-bearers. Such we must teach our church members to be; and without such an agency as our main dependence, we have little reason to expect the Gospel to prevail in China.

2. Elders must be "appointed in every city." This duty is enforced in Scripture, both by precept and example. Missionaries have not been backward in carrying out this injunction. It is possible that we have erred in the opposite direction. While the elders should be ordained as soon as practicable, we should not forget that the qualifications of elders are minutely laid down in the Scriptures; and to choose and ordain men to this office without the requisite qualifications is in the fact going contrary to, rather than obeying the Scriptures. If suitable elders are not to be found, we should wait for them, however long a waiting may be required.

The Apostolic usage of ordaining elders soon after their reception into the Church, under circumstances very different from ours in China, is apt to mislead us. The work of the Apostles in the heathen lands commenced for the most part in the synagogues of the Jews resident in those lands. Even in such places as Lystra, where there seems to have been no synagogue, there were Jewish families and their influence had been felt by the native population. Among the first converts to Christianity were both Jews and Jewish proselytes who for generations had been freed from the thraldom of idolatry. They were sincere worshippers of Jehovah, familiar with the Old Testament Scriptures and waiting for the long promised Messiah. From such persons the first elders of the Christian Church were no doubt largely drawn. It is not strange that, as a rule, we in China have to wait for years before Christians of the same intelligence and stability of character can be had. Our experience in this matter in Shan-tung is worth relating.

Twenty years ago our mission in considering this subject reasoned on this wise: We are Presbyterians, and our churches should be organized from the first on Presbyterian principles. If we cannot get men for elders as well qualified as we should like, we must take the best men we can find, men who seem sincere and earnest Christians, and who may develop in character and ability to fulfill the duties of elders by having the duties and responsibilities of this office laid upon them. With these views and expectations several churches were formally and constitutionally organized. It was found, however, in not a small proportion of cases that the elders did not, or could not, perform their official duties, and were an obstruction to any one else attempting to do so. They were placed in a false position, injurious to themselves and the churches of which they had the nominal charge. Some were hardly able to sustain the character of an ordinary church member and others were in the course of a few years excommunicated. We then took action as a Presbytery, determining that elders should not be appointed unless their qualifications conformed in some good degree to those required in Scripture. Perhaps we are now in danger of going to the opposite extreme of backwardness.

In central Shan-tung no church has as yet been organized with native elders, though some of our stations have had an existence with from ten to twenty and more church members for a period of seven or eight years. We are hoping very soon to ordain elders in some of these stations. In the meantime the leaders are unofficially performing many of the duties which will fall into the hands of elders when appointed. The missionary or evangelist in charge transacts all important business by consultation with the whole company of native Christians or their leaders. These Christians or leaders have only advisory power, the authority of deciding questions being vested solely in the missionary. It is his aim to instruct and train leading church members in the management of church business, developing it on them as they are able to undertake it, thus fitting them as soon as possible for assuming the care of the churches altogether. The missionary keeps a record of these meetings, following in almost all particulars the ordinary form of session records, and this report is presented to the Presbytery for examination and revision. Many of our present leaders will in all probability, after they have been fully trained and tried, become our first elders. We have found in the experience of the past eight years much reason for thankfulness that we did not ordain elders at an early period.

3. Our mission churches under the charge of elders are possessed of a Scriptural organization without the addition of a paid pastor, such as is found in most of our western churches; and the appointing of such a pastor might prove injurious rather than advantageous.

In enlarging on this point I will quote the language of Dr. Kellogg, formerly professor in the Theological Seminary at Allegheny, Pa. It has special weight as coming from one who is not only a highly esteemed theological teacher in our Church, but has been for years a missionary in India and has the advantage of large experience and observation of mission matters. The quotations are taken from an article in the "Catholic Presbyterian," November, 1879, page 347. Dr. Kellogg says:

"We fear there is reason to think that our missionaries have often been in too much haste to introduce the one-man pastorate of the European and American churches, and that the growth of a church bearing the true individual character of the particular people or race has been thereby seriously retarded. Fixed in the conviction that the primitive form of Church government was Presbyterian, men have apparently jumped to the conclusion that therefore the present form of Presbyterianism is the primitive and Apostolic arrangement,—a point, we may venture to affirm, which has not yet been established, nor is likely soon to be. Under this belief they have not only felt that if they established churches they must give them a Presbyterian form of government—in which they have been right—but that it must be that particular form of development of Presbyterian principles which has obtained among ourselves; wherein, as it seems to us, they have been as clearly wrong. For to take any one of our full-grown ecclesiastical systems and attempt to set it up bodily in our heathen fields, regardless of the widely differing conditions of the case, is, we submit, a great mistake. . . . In too many instances, the course pursued has proved a mistake by its practical working. . . .

But, it is asked with some confidence, What is the missionary to do? Shall we leave the young church without a pastor? We ask in reply, Where in the New Testament is there any intimation that the Apostles ordained pastors, in the modern sense of that word, over the churches which they formed? We read over and again of their ordaining "elders" in every church, and that, having done so, they left them and went elsewhere. Where is there the slightest hint that, at this early period, any one from among these elders was singled out and appointed by Paul to a position like that of the modern minister or pastor of a church, or that until such an officer was found they did not dare to leave the church?"

4. The appointment of elders should not interfere with the voluntary activities of church members. Rather than encourage such an idea I should postpone their appointment.

We are taught that, when our Saviour ascended on high, "He led captivity captive, and gave gifts unto men." "And he gave some to be apostles; and some, prophets; and some, evangelists; and some, pastors and teachers." Elsewhere we read of "exhorters," "workers of miracles," "speakers of tongues," "interpreters of tongues," "helps" and "governments," "gifts of healing," and "power to cast out devils." May we not confidently expect that the Divine Spirit will also confer special gifts upon the Church of the present, perhaps not the same as at first, but gifts suited to our times and circumstances as those of the early Church were to theirs? And should not our methods of church organization be such as to give the freest scope to the exercise of all special gifts conferred?

It is to be observed that in the gifts conferred on the early Church "elders" are not included. May it not be that this is because the "gifts" are special and variable, while the office of elder is fixed and permanent? It is not the function of the elder or overseer as such to assume and undertake wholly or mainly the work of the Church, but to encourage, direct, and assist all believers in the exercise and development of their special gifts as members of the one spiritual body of Christ; to set an example of working for all to imitate; to be leaders and captains in Christ's army, ruling, instructing, and directing those who are under their authority and care.

I am disposed to think that the tendency to make working for the Church the duty of office-bearers alone, rather than of all Christians, is introduced by missionaries from the Church at home. There is a prevailing disposition in western lands, noticeable in Protestant communions as well as in the Romish Church, to an all-pervading spirit of ecclesiasticism. The Church is regarded as an organization under the direction and superintendence of its proper officer or officers, whose function it is, for and on behalf of its members and the ecclesiastical judicatory over them, to undertake and administer all church matters. A church member has a quieting sense of having discharged his duty if he has contributed generously towards building a suitable church edifice and the support of a preacher, is always found in his place as a worshipper, and attends to the prescribed rites and observances of the Church. This spirit, wherever it is found, tends to formalism both in the clergy and the laity. While it is far too prevalent, and it is to be feared growingly so, we may well rejoice that it is by no means universal. There are not a few churches in which the main work of the pastor is to keep all under him at work. In such churches you will find individual growth and church growth, joy in God's service and influences for good extending to the ends of the earth.

May we not regard the religious activities which have during the present generation sprung up outside the Church, such as those connected with the Moody and Sankey work, Young Men's Christian Associations, also new methods for reaching the masses recently adopted in the English Church, and even the "Salvation Army," as legitimate protests and healthy reactions against the tendency which we are reprobating. Let us not, by allowing our church members to think that their chief duty is to contribute money to the support of their pastor and attend religious services, reproduce here in China one of the most reprehensible features of the Church at home.

5. Paid or salaried agents should only be added as the people want them and can support them.

Here we meet with the important Scriptural principle that teachers in the Church should look for help in temporal matters to those whom they teach. Many advantages spring from this relation of mutual dependence. As the pastor gives his time and energies to his people and watches for their souls as one who shall give account, his people naturally accept from him not only instruction but admonition and reproof. The fact that he depends upon them wholly or in part for his support gives them a reasonable claim upon his services, and to him a strong motive for the diligent and conscientious performance of his duties. When the native pastor is supported by the Foreign Board the advantages growing out of this mutual dependence between pastor and people are lost, and a one-sided and unnatural relation is introduced of people and pastor depending on foreign aid, which works evil rather than good.

The experience of the London Mission in Amoy is worthy of notice in this connection. In the year 1868 a debt of $100,000 made it necessary for the foreign society to retrench, and the native churches were forced, with great difficulty, however, and by degrees, to support their own pastors. That financial crisis is now, I believe, looked back to as a providential blessing. It developed the strength, independence and self-respect of the native Christians and was the beginning of a new era of progress. Is it not probable that there are other stations and other departments of mission work from which the withdrawal of foreign funds would prove in the end a blessing rather than a misfortune?

It does not follow from this principle of mutual dependence that the native pastor must necessarily receive a regular salary and full support from those to whom he ministers; the wisdom of the London Mission in insisting that they should, in the case above referred to, may possibly be questioned. In the early history of a station it may not be either necessary or desirable for the preacher or pastor to depend entirely on his flock for support, or to devote his whole time to their spiritual care and oversight. In the early history of the United States, and at present in the new settlements, the minister spent and still spends no inconsiderable portion of his time in secular labor for the maintenance of himself and family. Existing circumstances, both at home and on the mission field, may make it desirable for the good of the church and usefulness of the pastor that he should take the same course. The relation of mutual dependence and responsibility between the teacher and the taught may be fully expressed and the advantages arising from that relation secured by different degrees of help, according to the needs of the minister and the ability of his people.

6. The evils connected with the appointment and support of native pastors by foreign societies are such as to demand further consideration.

The same desire to stimulate and advance the work prompts the employment of paid evangelists in opening new fields and of paid preachers afterwards. The effect in both cases is, I believe, in the end the opposite of that intended. In the former case the injury to the cause develops earlier; in the latter it is entailed on future workers and goes down to successive generations. Here again I cannot do better than to quote further the language of Dr. Kellogg. In speaking of the importance of not employing and paying native pastors from the funds of foreign boards, he says:

"This plan [that of organizing churches without pastors in the modern sense of that term] would also meet the vexations, and—as it has proved in some missions that we could name—the hitherto insoluble problem of the support of a native pastor. The pecuniary question has been one of the main difficulties, thus far, in the establishment of independent churches in our foreign mission fields. It is plain that if a man be set apart to give his whole time to the pastoral care of a church, he is rightfully entitled to a full support. But where is this to be raised? Most of these young churches in India, China and Africa are very poor. Fix the stipend as low as we will, they are not able to pay it. Shall the Church in America or Europe supplement their contributions? This is often done, and to the inexperienced might seem a very simple and excellent solution of the difficulty; but, in fact, with this arrangement, difficulties only multiply. For example, what shall be the salary? If, as has often been done, it is fixed at a point much higher than the average income of the people, this works great mischief. It elevates the pastor unduly above the average condition of the people of his church. It degrades the ministry by making the pastorate an object of ambition to covetous and unworthy men. It makes the church, in many cases, despair, from the first, of reaching the position of self-support. A moderate salary they might in time hope to be able to pay of themselves; a high salary they, with good reason, look upon as unattainable. We affirm, without fear of contradiction, that no one thing has more effectively hindered the development of independent, self-sustaining native churches in many foreign fields, than the high salaries which, with mistaken wisdom, are paid to many of the native pastors and helpers from the treasuries of the home churches. Shall we then give a low salary? We shall not thereby escape serious difficulty. Men educated even as pastors commonly are in heathen fields feel that they are justly entitled to more; and when they hear of the hundreds of thousands which the churches at home contribute for the support of the Gospel and which are supposed to be at the disposal of the missionary, they will not and do not generally take kindly to the refusal to pay at a high figure. In this way and sad alienations often occur between the foreign missionary and his native helpers. In some parts of Northern India, in particular, this unhappy state of things is quite well known and formed the subject of earnest discussion at the Lahore and Allahabad conferences.[*]

"It appears to the writer that the root of all this trouble lies in the direction indicated. Have we not been trying to establish a form of Church government and organization, which, however well adapted to us, and however Scriptural in principle, is in advance of the position of the majority of our foreign mission churches? And is not this the real significance of these trying experiences in the matter of the native pastorate? On the apostolic plan of Church organization there would evidently be no room for trouble of this sort. Here and there, indeed, upon our mission fields, there may be a native church which, in wealth, intelligence and members is ready for the one-man pastorate; but we believe that, for the great majority of churches, which are weak and poor, the original Presbyterian system of rulership and instruction by a plural eldership is one form which is adapted to their need. The other will no doubt come in due time, but we act most unwisely in attempting to force it prematurely."

It may be urged as a further objection against the early appointment of native pastors over each church, that the assumption

---

[*] The Presbyterian Board has met with precisely the same difficulty in Persia.

of such a burden by a weak station while ill able to bear it renders it impossible for it to do what it ought, and otherwise could and would do, for others, and induces in its members a fixed habit of planning and laboring only for themselves. The sin of selfishness belongs to churches as well as individuals, and it always bears bitter fruit. We should guard against it from the first, teaching young converts that "there is that scattereth and yet increaseth;" that "it is more blessed to give than to receive," and that "those who water others shall be watered themselves." The first contributions of the early Christians which we read of in the New Testament were for others and not for themselves.

Experience Proves the Wisdom of Scripture Teachings.

Theories are very apt to mislead us; our safest guide is practical experience. Though our work in Shan-tung is still in its infancy, it will throw light on some questions of great importance.

1. It has been proved that the extension of country work and the establishment of new stations are practicable without paid preachers. The more than sixty stations under my care have been commenced within eight years almost exclusively through the voluntary efforts of unpaid church members. My helpers, who have never been at any one time more than four, have only followed up, fostered and directed the work begun by unpaid Christians.

2. These stations do not now need pecuniary aid from foreigners, and such aid would in my opinion do more harm than good. The leaders in charge, under the superintendence of the helper are, I think, caring for the stations as well as they could be cared for under the circumstances. If the plan should be adopted of providing paid preachers for each station, they would of necessity have to be chosen from the leaders, as there is not a sufficient supply of such men elsewhere. Paying them for their work would not increase their influence, but rather diminish it and would, no doubt, excite envy and dissatisfaction among the unemployed. Besides, the characters of these leaders are not sufficiently tested to warrant their being used in that way. The natives would, I think, be unwilling to make such a selection. If it should be attempted, they would probably divide into

parties influenced by personal motives, and the result would be great harm to the leaders and to the Church. Any change at present would in my opinion be premature and injurious, and we can only wait for future developments and Divine guidance.

3. These stations are not only able to provide for their own wants, with the superintendence which is given them, but could and ought to do much for the propagation of the Gospel in the regions beyond. They might easily contribute five hundred dollars a year. These Christians formerly contributed for idolatrous purposes probably double that amount; and if each church member should give one-tenth of his or her income, the yearly contribution for benevolent objects would not be less than two thousand dollars a year. As it is, they do not contribute one hundred and fifty dollars for benevolent purposes, aside from the necessary expenses of keeping up their own chapels. These facts show a manifest failure in duty on the part both of the foreign missionary and the converts.

The causes of this failure are various. First and foremost, no doubt, is the want of a cultivated habit of systematic giving. Another reason is the failure to set before the native Christians suitable objects to which they should contribute. Here perhaps the principal fault of the missionary lies. Having no pressing need for money in the conduct of these stations, and there being great danger to the natives in hoarding and manipulating money kept for future use, it was feared that an objectless contribution of money might only be a means of temptation and do harm. Last autumn the Christians in one of the *hsien* occupied by my stations, subscribed about sixty dollars for employing a helper to devote his whole time especially to the *hsien* and would, I think, have paid it cheerfully, if the right man could have been found; but neither they nor I could obtain a man whose gifts and qualifications, as compared to those already in charge, were such as to make him desirable.

During the last few years I have urged the stations to contribute to the support of the helpers, as the most natural and available object which could be presented to them. They have done so to some extent, but the plan has not worked well. They have very naturally regarded the helpers as my men and not theirs, since they are chosen and directed by me in the carrying out of my plans. Not only have they shown a discrimination to contribute to their support, but the helpers also are averse to receiving aid from them. I have been disposed to press the point against them, but during the past year have come to the conclusion that the instincts of the natives are perhaps right, and that my plan has been unnatural and impracticable. Here again we are led back by experience to the teachings of Scripture; as the Apostle Paul provided not only for his own wants, but also for those who were with him, and appealed to the churches to acknowledge the fact that none whom he had sent to them had received pay from them.

Rev. J. H. Laughlin is now assisting me in my country work and will, I trust, soon take entire charge of it. We are this autumn (1885) endeavoring to inaugurate the following plan from which we hope for good results: The Christians comprised within the bounds of each district or portion of each district, are to choose for themselves two men to go out as their representatives and, supported by them, to work for the evangelization of new districts. No change is to be made for the present in the relations and ordinary occupations of the men so used. They are to be away from their homes two months in the autumn and two in the spring, the times when both they and the people generally are at leisure and the weather is most favorable for traveling, and when absent are not to receive a salary, but only a sum to cover traveling expenses. We hope that in this way aggressive zeal and a habit of giving will be developed; that much may be accomplished in the way of evangelistic work; that the reflex influence on the stations may be helpful; and that from the persons selected year by year, men may be found who, after the necessary testing and sifting, may be advanced to more important and responsible positions in the future.

V. BEGINNING WORK

What has been written thus far presupposes a state of things in which there are native Christians to be organized into stations. We will next consider questions relating to work in new fields there where are neither stations nor inquirers.

To missionaries beginning such a work, without native converts or inquirers and without a knowledge of the language, many questions arise of the first importance. As the beginnings contain the seeds of future growth and development both for good and for evil, every step should be taken with deliberation and prayer. In addressing my younger brethren, I take it for granted that they will not be unwilling that I should use a considerable degree of freedom in detailing my own observations and experiences.

The Study of the Language.

1. It may well be a matter of congratulation that the newly arrived missionary is exempt for the first year or two from the pressure and responsibility of deciding the many questions of mission policy upon which he must form an opinion at a later period. Whatever department of work he may devote himself to in the future, there is no room for doubt that his first duty is to give his time and energies to the thorough acquisition of the language as a necessary prerequisite to usefulness in work of any kind. For this it is of the greatest advantage to be free, as far as possible, from cares and interruptions of every description.

2. It is very desirable to obtain the occasional assistance of some foreigner well versed in the language in guarding against mistakes which are almost sure to be made in pronunciation, aspirates and idioms. None of these should be neglected. It is well to know from the start that the ear has to be trained, as well as the vocal organs,

and that in discriminating and determining the sounds of the Chinese language one's own senses are not to be depended upon. It often happens, as two or three persons listen to the same vocal utterance, that each hears it differently, according to his individual habit or preconception. Of course all cannot be right. Where acknowledged authorities agree, if the learner follows his own ear in opposition to them, he will probably go astray in ninety-nine cases out of a hundred. Where authorities differ, it will generally be on comparatively unimportant points and it will be a matter of little consequence whether you follow one or the other.

3. Even the sounds of an intelligent native accurately heard and reproduced are not as sure a guide as a thoroughly elaborated and consistent classification of sounds like that found in Williams' Dictionary or Wade's Syllabary, or the dictionaries and phrase books representing the southern dialects of China. Variations of individual teachers from the standard pronunciation will probably be found to be localisms or personal peculiarities. The systems of pronunciation referred to are the result of the consensus of opinion of many foreigners, who may be regarded as experts, and of numerous trained natives, during a succession of many years or generations. A person may choose between Wade's system and Williams' in accordance with his purpose to speak the pure Peking Mandarin or a more general Mandarin. Either system is excellent and the differences between them are practically of little importance. They are much less than exist between the languages of many Chinese officials who can converse with one another without difficulty.

4. While it is no doubt desirable sooner or later to become acquainted with localisms, it is perhaps better at first to master the standard form of the dialect spoken, whether the Mandarin or any of the southern dialects. Localisms will be easy and almost unconsciously acquired afterwards as they are needed. Taking this course will secure a man's being generally intelligible; while those with whom he is constantly associated in his home, where his dialect may not be spoken in its purest form, will prefer to hear him speak without localisms rather than with them and will understand him almost if not quite as well. By adopting this course, church members would gradually become acquainted with and be able to use the standard form of their dialect, and thus indirectly the diffusion of

Christianity would promote uniformity in the language of people and as necessary consequence facilitate general intercourse.

5. A young missionary in acquiring the language should eagerly avail himself of all the "helps" at his command. Phrase books, grammars, dictionaries, a careful and well-trained native teacher, and the assistance and criticism of some foreigner are all important.

6. The native teacher should be made to understand that giving satisfaction to his employer and retaining his place depend on his laying aside Chinese ideas of deference and politeness, so far as they would prevent his correcting the same mistake of his foreign employer fifty times, if necessary, as it probably will be. It is a fact as common as it is unfortunate, that a teacher sometimes learns foreignized or individualized Chinese of the foreigner, who is led to suppose from the ease with which he is able to communicate with his teacher, that he is making rapid progress in the acquisition of the language, while he has unconsciously been playing a game with the Chinese teacher of "give and take." The result of this process is a kind of compromise between the English and the Chinese languages, made up of Chinese words with an admixture to a greater or less degree of foreign idioms, pronunciations, inflections, emphasis and aspirates, or want of aspirates. The extreme result of a similar process is found in the "Pidgin English."

7. Frequent changes in methods of study are sometimes desirable in order to break up monotony and avoid weariness. Each individual will learn by experience the particular way of prosecuting his studies which suits him best. Most persons find that from one to three hours a day with a Chinese teacher in getting correct sounds from his lips, are as much as can be spent profitably at first. The great work, that of memorizing words and sentences, can be done better quietly by one's self. When a good beginning has been made in pronunciation, tones and aspirates, only the occasional help of a foreigner is required. In the course of from six months to a year, most persons will find it very helpful to spend a good deal of time mainly or exclusively with natives, so as to force themselves to speak Chinese. At this period, a tour into the country or living for a time in the country without a foreigner, making a companion of one's personal teacher or a native preacher, is very useful.

In the course of a year or more, when one is able to converse with some freedom, it is generally desirable to change the teacher, as facility of communication with him will be partly the result, and that unavoidably, of a mutual adaptation to each other. A change of teachers, or talking a good deal with natives generally, will enlarge the learner's vocabulary and show him how far he has got on in acquiring the language as spoken by the people. With all the helps which can be obtained a man must depend mainly on regular, persistent, hard study. If he has a natural gift for languages it will of course be invaluable, but even this must not be trusted to as the chief dependence.

8. In the course of two or three years or more, the missionary may form a permanent or general plan of study for his lifetime. Some think it is best to confine their attention to the Chinese spoken language and regard an attempt to learn the written language or *wên-li*—with probably a very imperfect and unsatisfactory result—a useless waste of time, which might better be spent in mastering the vernacular and fitting themselves for effective preaching. One might indeed in this way save much time and also find a sphere of great usefulness, as a large proportion of the population of China is only acquainted with the spoken language. To reach all classes, however, and especially the influential classes, the knowledge of the *wên-li* is of immense advantage. It may be acquired in connection with a great deal of other work, if the study of it is prosecuted methodically and persistently and the missionary avoids burdening himself with so much and so many kinds of work as to make it impossible. I should strongly recommend from the first a regular exercise in writing characters and in memorizing select passages of the Classics.

Beginning Direct Missionary Work.

1. Here, if I mistake not, we are apt to be too hasty. After years of preparation at home we are anxious to begin our life work at once. We hardly realize that aside from the study of the language other special preparation for the work before us is still necessary. If a man has come from home designated to a particular department of work, or the exigencies of his field on his arrival constitute a call to some

special work, the case is quite different. If there is no such call I should, as a rule, advise him to keep clear from the responsibilities and distractions of an independent personal work for three, four or more years. One ought not to allow himself to be troubled with the thought that he is holding back and not taking his full share of labor, or with the fear that he may lay himself open to such imputations from others. I recommend this plan as the best course for securing the greatest usefulness. In the meantime, while the young missionary may not be able to point to any tangible results of work of his own, he may have the satisfaction of doing good from the first and that in many ways. He may bring a cheering gleam of sunshine from the home-land to those who are worn and weary and perhaps disheartened by the pressure of accumulated and exhausting toil. In leisure hours he can relieve other missionaries of some kinds of secular work which he can probably do as well as they, leaving them free to devote more time to work for which a knowledge of the language is a necessity. In a godly, unselfish, Christ-like walk, he may produce deep and lasting impressions for good, both on natives and foreigners, before he can begin to speak in the native language. As he advances in his knowledge of Chinese he can help his brethren in many ways, such as chapel preaching, teaching a class in a school, or accompanying and assisting older missionaries on itinerating tours. These kinds of work and all kinds of work, while they will be a help to others and the common cause, will be a still greater help to himself—just the preparation and training which he needs.

2. I should advise a young missionary when he has acquired the language or while he is still acquiring it, to visit different stations connected with his own mission and stations of other missions to acquaint himself by personal observation, as well as by a special course of reading, with the divers methods employed, and not to be hasty in forming opinions and acting upon them until he has gathered sufficient materials upon which to found these opinions.

3. The opposite course is liable to many objections. Confining one's self to the place where he is located, subject to one set of personal and local influences, forming opinions and acting on them at an early period, is apt to make a man narrow in the beginning and then confirm him in his narrowness. In taking up an individual work at an early period, he meets with difficulties and responsibilities

which he had not anticipated; a great deal of time is wasted in the laborious and imperfect performance at work which a few years later might be attended to with care and success. Plans for continued study, for which it was supposed plenty of leisure would be afforded, have to be given up in a consequence of pressure of engagements, pre-occupation of mind, or exhaustion of body. By undertaking work which one is incompetent to do and the difficulties of which one cannot anticipate, important interests are imperiled, injurious impressions produced which it is difficult to efface, and health and even life may be sacrificed. It has been to me a matter of constant regret that a portion of time was not strictly reserved, especially during my first five or ten years in China, for laying a broader and deeper foundation for future usefulness by a more extensive and methodical reading and memorizing of Mandarin and Classic literature. Suitable and adequate plans were made for such study, but other occupations in the form of direct missionary work, promising immediate results, were allowed to interfere with and set aside those plans. In this way, as in many others, we are too easily induced to sacrifice a greater future good to a less present one.

Independent Individual Work.

1. Though the time of preparation for individual work may have been somewhat protracted, the missionary will feel at its close that he is all too imperfectly fitted for the task before him. He must now, however, without unnecessary delay, take his full share of labor and responsibility. Before this point is reached, providential circumstances and personal tastes and proclivities will probably have indicated clearly his department of labor. This, while it should not be desultory, should not be too much specialized. A variety of work promotes physical and intellectual health. Employments may be so arranged and affiliated, that instead of interfering with each other, they may be mutually helpful. This is specially true of study, teaching, preaching, itinerating and book making. Each of these, in the above order, is a preparation for that which follows; and the succeeding ones, by their reflex influence, stimulate and assist those that precede. Missionary life must begin with study, but it should not

end there. All study or no study—too much study or too little—are extremes equally to be avoided. The results of study can only be assimilated and utilized by constant, familiar and sympathetic intercourse with the people, and people of all sorts.

2. If I were asked what in my opinion is the most important of all departments of mission work in China, I should not be able to answer categorically. All are important. The most important work for each man is undoubtedly that for which he is best fitted and to which he is specially called. Book-making is the ripest and richest fruit of all. Its influence goes down to successive generations. To consider the different departments of missionary work in detail would far transcend the limits assigned to these pages. One branch, however, Itinerating, claims our special attention, as particularly connected with the subject of the previous chapters.

Itinerating.

1. In engaging in this department of work we may certainly have the satisfaction of feeling that we are in complete accord with the great commission: "Go ye into all the world and preach the Gospel to every creature," and also with the example of the great Apostle to the Gentiles. While the active labors of this Apostle were largely made up of teaching, preaching and writing, itinerating may perhaps be regarded as their distinguishing feature and that to which he was specially set apart by the Holy Ghost.

2. The great centres where he spent most of his time were apparently not selected by him in accordance with a predetermined plan, but were providentially indicated to him in the ordinary course of his Apostolic tours. But most missionaries, however much they may itinerate, will require a fixed place of residence, that is a home, in selecting which the chief considerations should be health, facilities for acquiring the language, and a place which is an influential centre in itself and affords easy access to the evangelized regions about it. Such a home the Apostle Paul had at Antioch, where he spent the intervals between his itinerating tours.

3. When the time comes for practically answering the question, "How shall I make a beginning?" I should say, Do as the Apostle

did. Go everywhere preaching the Gospel. You can not know where there may be some one waiting for you and some one to whom you have been sent. Ask for direction. Christ's sheep will hear His voice. How shall we find them? Go everywhere "Christ's sheep" are, there they will respond to His call. Then you will have a beginning from which to work and one of God's own choosing.

Assistants or Helpers.

1. Our Saviour sent out his disciples on evangelic tours two by two. There are many special advantages to be gained in a foreigner being accompanied by a well-trained native helper, if such a one is to be had, the foreigner attracting an audience, while the Chinaman may possibly do most of the talking. Constant intercourse with a native not only, as has been remarked before, the best way to acquire a familiar and practical knowledge of the language and native character, customs and modes of thought, but it is also the best way for the foreigner to communicate to his assistant practical instruction to develop his Christian character and influence him for good. It is not easy, however, to find just such men as one would like, even in the older stations, and the young missionary may feel himself specially fortunate if he is able to obtain one.

Still, the work may be begun and prosecuted successfully without such a helper, and far better without one than with a person who is not a sincere and earnest Christian. Before the missionary is ready for itinerating he will probably have had in his employ for many months a personal servant who, though he may not be a convert, may be, if he is in sympathy with his employer, very serviceable on an itinerating tour. He will everywhere be the person applied to by the curious villagers to obtain all sorts of information about the character, mode of life and aims and purposes of the foreign visitor. Indeed, the fact that your attendant is not a professed Christian makes his countrymen all the more free in communicating with him and gives additional weight to his testimony.

2. If your servant has been brought to Christ while in your employ, the fulness and warmth of his testimony will more than compensate for the want of credence consequent on being a co-

religionist and as such pledged to speak for you. In an early period of my work in Ning-po, I had a Christian servant who was to me invaluable. He was a tailor by trade, and learned to be a good washerman and cook. After becoming a Christian he accompanied me on my tours, attending to my washing, mending and cooking, making himself generally useful, and at the same time was earnest and judicious in bearing witness to Christianity when opportunity offered. Most of those whom he met with were more easily reached by him than they could have been by a scholar, as they were nearer to him on the social scale and more in sympathy with him. I then felt, with the other members of the Ning-po mission, that he was too valuable a man to be employed as a servant, and he was induced to change his position in life and was employed successively as chapel-keeper, assistant, etc. I now think we made a mistake in not leaving him in the position of servant, and fear that he has never been as happy or useful since as he was in his original sphere of life.

3. Boatmen, cartmen, muleteers and wheel-barrow men in our employ, and inn-keepers with whom we stop, though not Christians, may be of great service to us, if their relations and dispositions towards us are such as to incline them to throw their influence in our favor. On the other hand, if they are prejudiced against Christianity, or cherish a feeling of resentment on account of real or fancied injuries, they may do us much harm. In fact, by their fault-finding, exaggerating real wrongs and repeating idle rumors, they may neutralize all our preaching. I once employed a muleteer who was an ill-tempered man and strongly prejudiced against Christianity. He, as I afterwards learned, reported wherever I went that the Chinese helper accompanying me was a cheat and a deceiver; and that moreover most of those who entered our religion soon become insane! That this trip was not a very satisfactory one in its results need not be a matter of surprise. I am glad to be able to say that my experiences have not always been of this kind.

About six years ago, I was detained in a small country inn by a severe case of persecution which was exciting a great deal of interest in the neighborhood. At the close of a busy day one of my wheel-barrow men came to me and said: "There is a man here who lives near my home about twenty miles away whom it would be well for you to have a talk with. He stopped here for lunch at noon, became interested in what is going on, and has questioned me the whole afternoon about you and what you are doing. He has remained so long that he cannot reach home today and will stay in the inn over night." In less than two years from that time this new acquaintance made a public profession of his faith in Christ. All the members of his family, which is a large one, are now Christians; his home has become an important Christian centre, and eight or ten stations have sprung up near his native town, mainly through his influence. These two wheel-barrow men are persons constantly in my employ, whether at home or on country tours. They are not as yet baptized and at that time were not specially inclined to become Christians. I often obtain from them important information respecting the villages through which I travel, and also hear from them faults and irregularities in my stations, some of which even the native helper has failed to discover.

How Shall We Reach the People?

1. When places in the interior are visited for the first time, there are opportunities to preach to crowds such as will probably never occur again. The whole population, moved by curiosity, comes out to see the foreigner, eagerly intent to hear what he has to say. In preaching under these circumstances, even when well acquainted with the language, we must not expect the people to understand more than a moiety of what we say. There is too much curiosity, excitement and noise to admit of connected discourse or continued attention. Besides, the people are so unaccustomed to religious subjects that language fails to communicate the idea intended. This kind of preaching, though for the reasons above stated very ineffectual as regards its main object, is still by no means unimportant. We may at least leave the impression behind us that we have kindly intentions, that we are not barbarians, and may also give some general idea of our character and work as religious teachers, thus preparing the way for a more lengthened visit and more detailed teaching in the future. We may also hope and pray that in the crowd which gathers around us as we pass from village to village, there may be some person prepared to receive our message, or that the

good seed may find a permanent lodgment in some heart and bring forth fruit hereafter. A few tracts are very useful at such a time to convey to the people, as they are read afterwards, better ideas of our object than we have been able under the circumstances to give orally.

2. There are many advantages in visiting the regular fairs, which are so striking a feature of country life in most parts of China. Here crowds of country people are gathered and an excellent opportunity is afforded for addressing a constantly changing audience, representing many surrounding villages and distant cities. If there are those listening who wish fuller instruction or whose curiosity is not satisfied, they will probably seek out the missionary at his inn.

3. In the inn there is an opportunity for more or less lengthened conversation, adapting instruction and information to individuals and forming acquaintances which may be followed up in the future. Books can also be disposed of with a greater degree of care and discrimination. In parts of the country where there are canals the traveling boat largely takes the place of the inn.

4. Visits to native schools are sometimes very interesting and encouraging. Here we may expect widely differing receptions and experiences according to the character of the teacher in charge.

5. Some missionaries adopt indirect and unobtrusive methods, avoiding crowds and making comparatively little use of public preaching, planning to have the people seek them, rather than going after the people. The Romanists, so far as my observation goes, generally adopt this method. Their long experience and success render their example worthy of serious consideration.

6. Others, wherever they go, make inquiries after religiously disposed persons or seekers after the truth, a class which is found in greater or less numbers almost everywhere in China, and endeavor to influence them and through them the circle of friends or adherents always found connected with them. This plan is obviously reasonable and practical and has the special sanction of our Saviour's teachings, Matthew X. II. It has been largely adopted by the English Baptists in Shan-tung and with encouraging results.

7. While the most missionaries give their chief attention to the middle or more illiterate class, a few feel a special call to attempt to influence the literati and officials, not only because they exercise a dominating influence on the masses, but also because they have been

in general too much neglected. It is obvious that this kind of work is attended with peculiar difficulty and requires special preparation, particularly in acquainting one's self with Chinese etiquette. Indeed, a theoretical and practical knowledge of Chinese rules of politeness is very important for every missionary in intercourse with all classes.

How Best To Expend One's Time?

In what way should we spend our time and talents so as to accomplish most for the advancement of Christ's cause?

1. The dominant idea of a missionary should be duty, and not immediate individual success as judged by human standards. If the desire for tangible results should take the form of a wish to gather into the Church as soon as possible the greatest number of professed converts it may become a dangerous temptation and snare.

2. It will be nearly fifty years hence to determine with positive certainty what any individual life has or has not accomplished. Only in eternity will every man's work be fully made manifest of what sort it is. Results of apparently great importance may attract attention and secure general commendation, and yet prove only temporary and illusory. On the other hand, a good book or a word spoken in season, may produce important results, though the world may never be able to trace them to their true source.

3. Probably no two men ever have or ever will work in the same groove. Each will do his own work best in his own way. If God has called us as individuals to serve Him in China, He has a special work for each of us to do, and if we earnestly seek His guidance He will direct us to it. It is apt to be a very different one from that which we have been disposed to plan for ourselves.

4. It is sometimes asked, what practical answer does the experience of missionaries in China for the past forty years give to the question, "Which methods of work have really brought the greatest number of converts into the Church?" This question is a legitimate and important one, but can only be answered approximately. The conventional modes of work which sum up the labors of missionaries as reported every year to the home societies

are Bible distribution, tract distribution, chapel preaching, translating and book-making, schools, and itinerations.

The number of copies of the Bible and parts of the Bible distributed in the different parts of China during the past forty years can only be estimated by millions; the same is true of Christian tracts.

Many missionaries have given their time largely to chapel preaching and have thus spent from one to three hours daily. A great deal of this work has also been done by natives. The number of chapel discourses during the past forty years can also be estimated by millions.

The result of literary work in the study cannot be tabulated. It passes into and is utilized in every other department of labor.

The aggregate number of years spent in teaching in the different kinds of schools during the last forty years, can only be numbered by thousands.

As to itinerations, it is a very common thing for a missionary to preach in from five to ten villages in a day and from two hundred to five hundred times on a tour. The number of these itinerating addresses during these forty years can only be numbered by hundreds of thousands, and, including those of natives, probably by millions.

The question is, To which of these different modes of work is the conversion of the about 30,000* Protestant Christians of China to be mainly traced? I am disposed to think that the number of conversions due to each would be found to increase about in the order in which they are mentioned above; that the number traceable to them all together would be but a small fraction of the whole; and that by far the greater proportion is to be referred to private social intercourse. "The Kingdom of God cometh not with observation."

---

* The present number of Protestant communicants is 80,862.

Missionaries but Instruments in Spiritual Work.

In the spiritual work of the conversion of souls and building up Christ's Kingdom on earth, we of ourselves can do nothing but except as instruments.

1. This is a fact so familiarly known and universally acknowledged that it may well be regarded as a simple truism. Theoretically, we learned this lesson almost in infancy; practically, it is difficult for some of us fully to learn it in a lifetime. It is so natural for us to feel that with a good knowledge of the language, sincere earnestness and sympathy with the people, together with prudence, common sense, zeal, hard work and perseverance, sooner or later great spiritual results must certainly be accomplished. This is by no means the case. Our labors may combine all the above conditions and yet be fruitless in the conversion of souls. If we depend upon our gifts or acquisitions, our zeal in the use even of God's appointed means, with an underlying and insidious desire for a result which may be regarded as something which we ourselves have accomplished, we shall probably be disappointed. If we are cherishing a feeling of self-dependence in any form, God will probably humble us before He will use us. We must feel that if anything is accomplished it will be by the presence and power of God's Holy Spirit, and be ready to ascribe all the glory to Him. Otherwise He will probably leave us to ourselves to learn the lesson of our own weakness. The natural tendency to depend on self, or on anything else rather than God, has been a prominent sin of God's people from the earliest times. I am disposed to think that this tendency now prevails to a great extent among Christians at home and that missionaries commence work in foreign lands too much under the influence of it.

2. In this commercial age a commercial spirit has crept into the Church. As in business matters generally, so in religious enterprises, it is supposed that a certain amount of capital, judiciously expended, will naturally work out a certain result. The success of a mission society is gauged by the amount of money in its treasury. In order to secure more liberal contributions, only the more favorable and encouraging facts are welcomed and laid before the churches, so that

they may feel that they are contributing not to a failing but to a prospecting cause. Let me not be understood as implying that money is not important and that the duty of giving to missions should not be pressed home upon the hearts and consciences of all, whether native converts or home Christians. The danger I would guard against is of giving such disproportionate prominence to money as to divert the mind from what is of much greater importance. In a word, it is making money or what money can command, rather than the Holy Spirit, our main dependence. I am quite aware that all Christians would earnestly disavow any such intention. It is not an uncommon thing, however, to find ourselves doing indirectly, or unconsciously, what we could never be induced to do deliberately and knowingly. The work we are prosecuting is distinctly and emphatically a work of God's spirit. If we fail to recognize and act upon this fact, the mission work will decline even with a full treasury; while with the Spirit's presence it will prosper even with a depleted one.

Personal Experience in Beginning Work in Shan-Tung.

1. I commenced itinerating work in Central Shan-tung about fifteen years ago, my previous tours having been in the eastern part of the province. I knew the language and had the advantage of seventeen years of experience elsewhere, but was without a native assistant. I prosecuted the work laboriously, making long tours over the same ground every spring and autumn, but for five years had not a single convert. The work at that time was quite different from what it is at present. Then my labors were entirely with the previously unreached masses, and consisted in preaching at fairs, in inns and on the street, in book distribution and efforts to form acquaintances with well disposed persons wherever I could find them.

2. At present nearly all my time and strength, when in the country, are expended on the native Christians on the plan detailed in previous chapters. As a rule, I now reach the masses indirectly through the Christians; they doing the aggressive work, and I following it up, directing and organizing it. Had I again to begin work in a new field, I do not know where I should change the

methods heretofore adopted, except in the one particular of not encouraging in any way hopes of pecuniary help.

3. Why these methods proved fruitless for so long a time it is impossible to say. In looking back over my experiences during the first five years of work in this field, it appears made up chiefly of failures and disappointments. Men for whom I had watched and labored for years, who seemed almost persuaded to be Christians, went back and were lost sight of. Associations of co-religionists were at different times on the point of entering the Church in a body with their leaders. From them all I have realized little else than wasted time and labor, with no doubt the acquisition of some valuable experience. I have in mind several places within my circuit where there seemed to be an unusual religious interest springing up, places which I hoped would soon be centres of Christian influence with chapels and native leaders; but these expectations have hardly been realized in a single instance. In some cases I have endeavored to encourage and stimulate persons who have been doing something in the way of active Christian work by giving them a little pecuniary assistance, hoping that they might be of help to me in the future. This class has not furnished, so far as I can recall, a single individual who has not disappointed me. Help in the way of pay for Christian work which ought to be done without pay has always done harm. The amount of pecuniary help which I have considered reasonable and ample in these cases has been regarded by beneficiaries as insufficient, and has often produced dissatisfaction, complaint and resentment.

4. When converts have appeared, they have come from unexpected quarters and in unexpected ways; stations have been established without my planning and in places previously entirely unknown to me. As a rule the now existing stations are not found in the sections of country where the itinerating work began, nor are the results realized directly traceable to previous work of seed-sowing. If asked the cause of the difference in the outcome of labors of the preceding and succeeding years, the question is not easy to answer. The influence of the work of famine-relief and a supposed special susceptibility to religious impressions in the regions where these stations are found will account but in part for the difference. We can only say that God in His inscrutable providence has so ordered it.

For myself, I have learned that God's ways are very different and infinitely wiser than mine; that it is better to follow than to take the lead; and that there is need to pray, not only that we may be used as instruments in God's work, but we may be kept from marring and obstructing it.

5. I might add here that I have known of many instances in which individuals and groups of individuals have been brought into the Church with very imperfect and erroneous views of Christianity, and moreover influenced largely by mercenary motives, who have afterwards given evidence of having become intelligent and sincere Christians.

6. Some have supposed that we are warranted in the first presentation of Christianity in withholding those doctrines which antagonize Chinese systems and are calculated to excite prejudice and opposition, presenting only those features which are conciliatory and attractive, thus drawing the people to us and gaining an influence over them and afterwards giving them instruction in the complete system of Christian truth as they are able to hear it. I doubt very much whether such a course is justified by the teaching and example of our Saviour and the Apostles. God may and does in His mercy and grace make use of our incomplete presentation of His truth and an imperfect apprehension of it to the conversion and salvation of men; but have we not still greater reason for expecting His blessing in connection with His truth when given its completeness? I believe there is no doctrine of Christianity the full presentation of which we need fear. With all our care to "declare the whole counsel of God" there will still be a great amount of misconception in the minds of those who hear us, and we may well be thankful that God will use and bless inadequate conceptions of His truth. It is for us, however, to make our teaching as full and clear as possible.

How May We Best Get Out of "Old Ruts"?

1. To those who still prefer the Old System this question has of course no relevancy, but it is presumed that there are others who will regard it as a practical and important one. In some respects it is much simpler and easier to commence work from the beginning. On the

other hand, there are many advantages in having an old foundation to build on and much good material to use. Many of our native employés sustain characters beyond reproach or suspicion. Some are efficient workers; others are simply out of their place, having been brought into a position for which they are unsuited and by long continuance in which they have become unfitted for their original modes of life. If there are any persons who are to be blamed for this result they are mainly the missionaries of twenty, thirty, or forty years ago, who inaugurated the present state of things, or the societies which sent them out with instructions to do so. Probably blame should be attributed to no one, as both foreigners and natives concerned have done what they regarded as their duty and what they supposed was for the best interests of the mission cause. Under these circumstances long established relations should not be rudely severed, and the natives, who are more to be pitied than blamed, should be treated with sympathy and justice.

2. In the case of competent and efficient pastors whose people are able and desirous to support them, no change is required. Other pastors, able and willing to "endure hardness," might take the charge of several weak churches which combined would be able to give them a competent support. Pastors left without charge by this union of churches might be employed, if they have the requisite gifts, as evangelists, either in opening new fields not yet reached, or in superintending weak and scattered companies of Christians who are under the immediate instruction of leaders and elders. Such evangelists, if thoroughly proved and tried, might be supported wholly by the mission or wholly by the native churches or by two conjointly. Others specially suited for the purpose might supply the helpers and attendants required by the new plan as well as the old. These would be connected with and under the direction of the missionary, giving him needed assistance in receiving, entertaining and instructing guests and inquirers, in itinerating tours, and in the care and oversight of inquirers and new stations. Others unfitted by age or incapacity for active service might be retired on a pension and left to do what they can by voluntary labor as private Christians. Assistance might be given to others for two or three years in acquiring some trade or profession. One of the older missionaries in China, much interested in this question, has suggested the plan of

furnishing to suitable men three years of theoretical and practical instruction in the science of medicine, thus putting within their reach a useful and honorable means of livelihood and then leaving them to themselves. By some means as this men of the right stamp might have their influence for good greatly enhanced.

3. Probably some readers of the foregoing pages may derive the impression that the writer is desponding and pessimistic in his views of mission work. On the contrary, if I may be allowed an opinion on such a question, I think I have always been rather sanguine, if not enthusiastic. I believe that much has been accomplished in every department of missionary work in China. The literary outcome of the past forty years is alone and by itself a rich legacy to the missionaries and native Christians of the present, and gives them a vantage ground in undertaking future labor which it is difficult to overestimate. The ratio of increase in the number of converts, and the evidence of growth and development in native churches, are also full of encouragement. While we must record many cases of coldness and defection, we remember that such cases have characterized the history and progress of the Church to a greater or less extent in every age. On the other hand, we rejoice in being able to point to many who give undoubted evidence of being God's chosen ones, while there are others whose names are already enrolled among the noble army of martyrs. It has been my privilege to know many Christian men and Christian women in China whose godly lives and peaceful deaths have been an inspiration to me and made me, I trust, a better man and a more earnest worker. I count among my nearest and most honored friends not a few native Christians who are now bearing faithful testimony to the truth in the midst of opposition and manifold trials such as Christians in Western lands can only imperfectly appreciate. It has been the object of these chapters, not to extol the virtues of Chinese Christians, concerning which volumes might be written, but rather to point out certain evils in what I regard a mistaken policy of missionary work. If the reader has not met with many reassuring facts and cheering prospects, it is only because this is not the place to look for them.

4. Thankfully acknowledging what has already been done, I believe we have not accomplished what we might if we had followed more closely the teachings and examples given us for our guidance

in the Scriptures. I believe that the injudicious use of money and agencies depending on money have retarded and crippled our work and produced a less self-reliant and stalwart type of Christians than we otherwise should have had.

5. I should exceedingly regret if the statement just made or any other statement in these letters should be understood or construed as intimating that the use of money in carrying on missionary work is not legitimate. In the nature of things pecuniary aid is an absolute necessity, not only for sending out and supporting well qualified and accredited missionaries, but also for hospital and dispensary work, for the preparation and dissemination of Christian literature, for establishing higher institutions of learning and for furnishing, as needed, grants-in-aid for primary or preparatory Christian schools. In supplying the funds thus required all Christians have the opportunity of sharing in the privileges and self-denials of the work of preaching the Gospel to every creature. Far more money is needed for the actual demands of the work than has hitherto been given. Some parts of the heathen world now fully open to missionary effort have scarcely been touched. In other places, like China, where the work has begun, the supply of laborers is utterly inadequate. If we refrain, as I have strenuously urged, from spending money in ways not sanctioned by the Scriptures and experience, we shall have the more to use in legitimate methods. Moreover, the Church, when fully satisfied that its contributions are wisely disbursed, will naturally be more spontaneous and generous in its liberality.

6. There are abundant evidences of God's willingness to bless our labors, and evidences also that the Gospel of Christ is as well adapted to the Chinese as to any other race. Let us, then, with unwavering faith in God's revealed Word and an implicit trust in the efficacy of the Divine Spirit, address ourselves to our labors with renewed zeal and earnestness; praying the Lord of the harvest to send forth laborers into His harvest and for the abundant outpouring of the Spirit upon us and those to whom we are sent; hoping and believing that in these most remote regions of Eastern Asia, so long preserved by God's providence, so thickly peopled with His erring children, and so lately reached by the message of salvation, the Church may yet record such signal triumphs of grace and power as have not been witnessed in any previous period of her history.

Made in the USA
Coppell, TX
07 January 2020